HOW TO RAISE SPOILED KIDS

A PARENT'S GUIDE TO GENERATIONAL WEALTH

DERRICK & TARIA SLACK

How to Raise SPOILED Kids:
A Parent's Guide to Generational Wealth

Copyright © 2025 by Derrick and Taria Slack

All rights reserved. No part of this book may be reproduced, stored in a retrieval system, or transmitted in any form or by any means—electronic, mechanical, photocopying, recording, or otherwise—without prior written permission of the publisher, except in the case of brief quotations embodied in critical articles or reviews.

First Edition, 2025

Published by

Black Leaf Publishing an imprint of KnoWonder Publishing
Indianapolis, Indiana, USA

ISBN: 978-0-9828657-9-8

Cover and interior design by Yasir Nadeem

Printed in the United States of America

This book is a work of nonfiction. While every effort has been made to ensure accuracy, the authors and publisher assume no responsibility for errors or omissions, or for the interpretations of the information contained herein. The advice and strategies included may not be suitable for every individual or family. Readers should consult with professionals where appropriate.

For information about permissions, inquiries,
or bulk purchases, please contact:

Black Leaf Publishing
manager@MySPOILEDKids.com

www.MySPOILEDKids.com

DEDICATION

To our daughters: Zyla, Zyon, and Zenaya. You are the heartbeat of our dreams and the reason behind every late night and early morning. This book is for you, and for every child who dares to believe that generational wealth is more than money—it is freedom, wisdom, health, and legacy.

And to our parents and ancestors—who planted seeds of resilience, faith, and love that continue to grow through us.

ACKNOWLEDGMENTS

This book could not have come to life without the unwavering love, patience, and encouragement of our family. To our girls, thank you for reminding us daily why generational wealth is not only possible, but necessary. You inspire us to build, teach, and share with courage.

To our extended family, friends, and community — thank you for holding us accountable to the vision of leaving a legacy bigger than ourselves. Your encouragement, prayers, and wisdom guided us when the journey felt long.

To the educators, mentors, and parents who are doing the hard work every day of shaping the next generation—this book is as much yours as it is ours. May it serve as a resource, a reminder, and a call to action.

And finally, to every reader: thank you for trusting us with your time and your dreams. Our hope is that this book will not just inform you, but empower you to create a life and a legacy of abundance that will endure for generations to come.

With gratitude,

Derrick & Taria Slack

TABLE OF CONTENTS

INTRODUCTION XII

PART 01 SAVERS 3

SAVERS 1.1: WHAT IS MONEY? 8

SAVERS 1.2: BUILDING A SAVERS MINDSET 12

SAVERS 1.3: NAME YOUR MONEY 15

SAVERS 1.4: BREAK GOALS DOWN 18

SAVERS 1.5: UNDERSTAND YOUR SPENDING HABITS 22

SAVERS 1.6: PRACTICE DELAYED GRATIFICATION 26

SAVERS 1.7: REWARD SMALL WINS 29

SAVERS 1.8: VISUALIZE YOUR FINANCIAL FUTURE 32

SAVERS 1.9: FINANCIAL LITERACY 35

SAVERS 1.10: UNDERSTAND COMPOUND INTEREST 37

SAVERS 1.11: CREATE A SAVER'S NETWORK 40

SAVERS 1.12: PLAN FOR UNEXPECTED EXPENSES 42

PART 2: PRODUCERS 45

PRODUCERS 2.1: CULTIVATING A

PRODUCER'S MINDSET 52

PRODUCERS 2.2: ENCOURAGE CREATIVE
PROBLEM-SOLVING 54

PRODUCERS 2.3: GOALS FOCUSED ON CREATION,
NOT CONSUMPTION 56

PRODUCERS 2.4: NEW SKILLS OVER BUYING
SOLUTIONS 60

PRODUCERS 2.5: CELEBRATE PROCESS,
NOT JUST RESULTS 63

PRODUCERS 2.6: ENCOURAGE EXPERIMENTATION
AND RISK-TAKING 68

PRODUCERS 2.7: DESIGN THINKING 71

PRODUCERS 2.8: TEACH THE VALUE OF
CONTRIBUTING TO COMMUNITY 75

PRODUCERS 2.9: BUILD AN "IDEA BANK" 79

PART 3: OWNERS 81

OWNERS 3.1: OWNERSHIP MINDSET 88

OWNERS 3.2: OWNERSHIP TAKES CASH 94

OWNERS 3.3: SHIFTING FROM PROTECT
TO PREPARE 100

OWNERS 3.4: DEBT FREE THINKING 107

OWNERS 3.5: THE BEST METHOD FOR FINANCIAL
FREEDOM 112

OWNERS 3.6: BUDGETING 116

OWNERS 3.7: ELIMINATING DEBT LANDSLIDE.........121
OWNERS 3.8: SACRIFICE 128
OWNERS 3.9: TIME..132

PART 4: INVESTORS 137

INVESTORS 4.1: THE INVESTOR MINDSET................142

INVESTORS 4.2: OUR INVESTMENT
LESSON 149

INVESTORS 4.3: THE GREATEST
INVESTMENT!..153

INVESTORS 4.4: MISPLACED
INVESTMENTS 157

INVESTORS 4.5: THE INTENTIONAL
NOW 161

INVESTORS 4.6: THE $86,400 INVESTMENT.............166

INVESTORS 4.7: A LIFE OF TRUE WEALTH 172

INVESTORS 4.8: INVESTING IN
BODY, MIND, AND FUTURE...178

INVESTOR 4.9: ASSETS AND LIABILITIES 181

INVESTORS 4.10: THE ASSET MINDSET......................189

PART 5: LEADERS 193

LEADERS 5.1: OUTWARD LEADERSHIP......................199

LEADERS 5.2: SITUATIONAL LEADERSHIP 204

LEADERS 5.3: SERVANT LEADERSHIP........................211

LEADERS 5.4: TRANSFORMATIONAL LEADERSHIP ..218

LEADERS 5.5: VISIONARY LEADERSHIP 223
LEADERSHIP 5.6: PASSIVE INSPIRATION - LEADING BY BEING 228

PART 6: ENTREPRENEURS 235

ENTREPRENEURS 6.1: THE ENTREPRENEURIAL MINDSET 240
ENTREPRENEURS 6.2: THE IDEAL IDEA...........246
ENTREPRENEURS 6.3: ENTREPRENEURS ARE LEADERS 252
ENTREPRENEURS 6.4: FEAR VS FAILURE 257
ENTREPRENEURS 6.5: THE POWER OF A SIMPLE STAND 261
ENTREPRENEURS 6.6: THE BLACK LEAF VEGAN STORY 264

PART 7: DISCIPLINE 269

DISCIPLINE 7.1: THE 4 CORNERS OF DISCIPLINE....274
DISCIPLINE 7.2: THE QUIET GENIUS 278
DISCIPLINE 7.3: YOU ARE WHAT YOU DO MOST 281
DISCIPLINE 7.4: SHAPING THE ENVIRONMENTAL ..286
DISCIPLINE 7.5: THE SEEDS OF DISCIPLINE 289
DISCIPLINE 7.6: THE GROWTH OF THE SEED..........294
DISCIPLINE 7.7: THE ROOT SYSTEM OF DISCIPLINE 296
DISCIPLINE 7.8: THE FRUIT OF DISCIPLINE..............300

DISCIPLINE 7.9: DISCIPLINE AS LEGACY....................303
CONCLUSION: LIVING THE SPOILED LEGACY........307

INTRODUCTION

Having children can be an exciting, rewarding, yet, at times, very frustrating endeavor. There are so many aspects of parenthood that must be managed, planned and considered carefully, all while often keeping a brave and calm demeanor so as to not appear as though we are cracking under the pressure that this wonderful assignment brings. We often say amongst ourselves, half-jokingly of course, how surprised we are that people have children at all given the multitude of challenges and the fear that accompanies keeping them safe, protected, and nurtured in a world that is often unpredictable. It is certainly a job best suited for the brave, the daring, and most prepared.

As first-time parents, we quickly realized how enormous a task we had undertaken. A tiny life now depended on us for everything: her safety, her growth, her sense of security, and her thriving. The weight of that responsibility felt immense, yet the love we felt drove us forward. We recognized that everything she would learn, every value and skill she would acquire, would be shaped largely by the foundation we provided.

Wanting the best for our child, we pulled from every source of wisdom available to us. We recalled lessons taught and caught from our parents, wise friends, mentors, and members of our community, piecing together what we believed to be the essentials of a loving, caring, and nurturing home. We learned quickly that parenting is an art as much as it is a science, a balance of providing structure while also fostering freedom, of guiding with principles while adapting to each new phase. And in each challenge, we found ourselves growing just as much as our child was growing, discovering that parenting, in many ways, reshapes us as we shape our children.

When we became parents in 2009, the world seemed quite a scary place. The global economic recession had left millions reeling; businesses were shutting down daily, and job losses were surging to levels not seen in generations. The housing market collapsed, leaving entire neighborhoods dotted with foreclosures and families scrambling for shelter. The stock market was failing, and with it, decades of savings were wiped out almost overnight, pushing many into a financial abyss. Unemployment soared to its highest levels in decades, leaving people struggling to cover inflated mortgages, rising living costs, and the ever-increasing price of childcare.

Beyond the economic turmoil, there was a storm of social and cultural strife. People from all walks of life were marching and protesting, demanding basic rights and recognition in a society that seemed more divided than ever. Many were fighting for marriage equality, immigration reform, and healthcare access, only to face opposition from state legislators determined to turn back the clock. The voices calling for justice were not only ignored but actively suppressed in some cases.

A new president had just taken office, embodying an historic moment that carried the promise of change, yet also unleashed deep-seated prejudices and divisions. Racial tensions, which many had hoped were easing, flared instead as unresolved resentments resurfaced, creating a hostile climate that only heightened our concerns as new parents. Wars and conflicts abroad continued, environmental catastrophes grew more frequent and the world as a whole felt more volatile and unpredictable.

Raising a child amid all this was daunting, to say the least. We felt acutely aware of the fragile balance we would need to strike, raising our child to be resilient and hopeful even as we felt our own foundations tested.

Yet, even amid the uncertainty, we held onto hope that our child—and any children that would follow—might still inherit a world filled with promise, wonder, and boundless opportunities. We wanted them to have a life of unbelievable joy, enriched by diverse experiences and perspectives from every corner of the globe, and a deep sense of security, free from the weight of social, political, cultural, or financial anxieties. We believed their world could be better. But as time passed, we came to realize how insufficient it was to simply hope for change; hope alone wasn't enough to make it happen. Real change would require deliberate action, and it would have to start with us.

For the world to change, we had to change—our thoughts, our habits, and the way we interacted with the world. We needed to show our children, through example, what it meant to live with intention, resilience, and a mindset grounded in possibility. Committed to making this vision a reality, we knew that we had to equip them not only with a mentality of opportunity and hope but also with a practical psychology that would enable them to turn dreams into plans and aspirations into achievements.

This meant teaching them about the value of faith and spirituality, providing a foundation of principles that could sustain them when life's challenges inevitably came. Just as importantly, we wanted them to know that they could create opportunities for themselves rather than waiting for others to pave their way. Our commitment to their future wasn't only about preparing them for a constantly changing world; it was about empowering them to be change-makers in that world.

With this in mind, we set about instilling in them the skills of adaptability, discipline, and the confidence to take initiative. Our goal was to raise children who wouldn't just experience life but who would engage with it fully—meeting each challenge with courage and each opportunity with gratitude. We wanted them to believe not only in the vastness of what the world has to offer but also in their own potential to contribute meaningfully to that world.

People often tell us that our children are "spoiled." They comment on the unique opportunities and experiences our daughters enjoy, experiences they believe are rare for children in their demographic. And maybe they're right—because, in many ways, our daughters are growing up with the world at their fingertips. But to us, this is not about spoiling them; it's about opening their eyes to the incredible vastness of the world and equipping them to navigate it with confidence, curiosity, and gratitude.

When each of our daughters reaches the age of ten, she embarks on a "10-Trip" with Dad—a special journey to any destination of her choosing anywhere on Earth. Our first daughter chose a life-changing trip to Dubai and Ghana, where she encountered new cultures and landscapes that would stay with her forever. Our second daughter, with a passion for animals, wanted to see elephants up close in Thailand, with a memorable stop in Japan to explore its unique traditions and sights. Not to be outdone, our third daughter aimed high, deciding she would be the first of the three to step onto her sixth continent with an unforgettable adventure in Australia. Each journey was filled with discovery, bonding, and awe—a gift that can never be wrapped but is priceless in its impact.

When they turn thirteen, it's time for the "13-Trip" with Mom, a new chapter of exploration. Our daughters have traveled to Jamaica Costa Rica, and Cairo, immersing themselves in vibrant cultures and natural beauty, learning firsthand the art of respect, compassion, and curiosity. And at sixteen, each child receives a "16-Trip" with both mom and dad and the one child—each trip creating memories that go far beyond any birthday or holiday gift could bring. In fact, we stopped giving gifts at holidays altogether. Instead, we give the gift of experiences, choosing to explore the world together as a family. We've traversed to the Grand Canyon, Yellowstone National Park, Gulf Shores, Crazy Horse, Rocky Mountains and many other places throughout the United States. We have ventured to Canada, Puerto Rico, the United Kingdom, South Korea, France, Zimbabwe, Zambia, South Africa, Kenya, Thailand, Vietnam, the Bahamas, Peru, Brazil, and so many other incredible places on six continents around the world, each trip adding a chapter in our family's story.

Of course, each of these trips comes with a lesson. Our daughters learn that these opportunities come from their own efforts as well as ours. They save to contribute to each adventure, working in one of our businesses, producing crafts to sell, or doing odd jobs for family. They learn the value of responsibility, resourcefulness, and the satisfaction of seeing their efforts come to life in the form of a plane ticket and a world of new experiences. So far, each has traveled to more than a two dozen countries—and their journey has just begun.

Then there's the milestone of sixteen: the year when they receive not a car but an income-producing rental property. We teach them to manage it, handle its expenses, and use the passive income as a foundation for their future. This income becomes a seed, growing as they save, invest, and reinvest, preparing them to build wealth, fund their dreams, and pursue education or new adventures. With each decision, they gain an understanding of financial independence, appreciating the power of owning something meaningful and the possibilities it brings.

And beyond trips and investments, they're active stakeholders in our businesses. They join us at the table for key decisions, gaining a sense of ownership, pride, and responsibility. They're growing up knowing that their ideas matter and that they have the power to shape their own futures.

So, are they spoiled? Maybe. But we see them as deeply enriched. They're learning that the world is theirs to explore, understand, and give back to, not simply as consumers but as contributors. They're learning that life is as vast and beautiful as they choose to make it, and that they have the power, knowledge, and experience to create a life full of purpose and wonder.

Perhaps our children are spoiled. Maybe we are exposing them to things and experiences their peers may not, or cannot do. Maybe what others call spoiled, we simply view as conscious decisions we are making to not cave to the pressures of how the world operates. We are not going to conform to the generational cycle of financial insecurities that our parents experienced. We are not going to allow our children to know a mindset of scarcity. We are normalizing for them to only know a world full of abundance, possibility, limitlessness. We want them to rise above any temporary economic condition and remain disciplined and committed to the paths that lead to wealth generation. We want to create a sense of self-agency and advocacy, to accept help, but never ever expect it. Saving themselves is solely their responsibility. We want them to value education and know the difference between it and school. We want to give them the ability to create and manifest any experience, any hope, any dream, any place on earth they desire to be.

Some may think that our way of raising our children is doing them a disservice by not allowing them to "figure it out the hard way" like generations before us. You know, the proverbial, "we had to walk three miles to school uphill both ways in the snow with no shoes on" character building speech. The "in my day, my parents had me swim across the lake because bridges made you soft" sentiment. The "back when I was your age, I wouldn't dare say that or do that" talk. OK, Boomer! Although there is tremendous value in the hard fought lessons of yesterday, we believe that there is no reason for our children to have to start the race all over again. Instead, we are choosing to pass the baton of bravery, prosperity, and economic safety to them as they relay their way to wealth.

This is why we're envisioning and executing plans to prepare our children for a life where they don't just get by but thrive—and thrive through their own hard work. From a young age, they're learning what it means to show up, put in effort, and solve problems independently. We want them to own several businesses not because it's easy, but because running a business teaches them the reality of long hours, difficult decisions, and the satisfaction of earning every dollar. We're shaping within them a worldview that tackles societal problems through an entrepreneurial lens, showing them that when challenges arise, it's not about waiting for someone else to fix things; it's about stepping up and creating the solution.

They are expected to manage multiple income-producing properties, understanding that each property requires diligence and a hands-on approach. Whether it's budgeting for repairs, negotiating with tenants, or preparing for inevitable unexpected expenses, they're learning that there's no room for shortcuts. There are no "quick wins"—only consistent work that, over time, builds lasting financial stability. And along with their properties, they're expected to maintain adequate savings for emergencies. We're not just talking about a rainy-day fund, but a mindset that understands the value of preparedness, resourcefulness, and always having a buffer when times get tough.

We also want them to see the world and gain perspective through cultural excursions, teaching them that hard work goes beyond making money. It means respecting different cultures, learning from diverse experiences, and developing an open mind that values service to others. We desire to instill the knowledge and skill to create money even when the odds are stacked against them. We're teaching them to be positive, outwardly-minded servant leaders who step up for their communities—not because it's easy or because anyone is watching, but because it's what builds real character.

Their mindset won't settle for a box that limits them to a traditional career path or a single source of income. They're expected to think outside of the box that confines many to complacency, to never stop learning, adapting, and creating new streams of income. We're teaching them to be investors who work intelligently and patiently, knowing that nothing worth having comes overnight. They're not just chasing profits; they're reinvesting in underserved communities, understanding the responsibility they hold to give back and recycle their success to create new opportunities for others.

We envision for them physical, emotional, mental, and financial stability, grounded in the resilience that only hard work can build. No longer is it necessary to build resilience by "walking barefoot in the snow uphill both ways," but what we are providing for them definitely is no "walk in the park" either. Some may think they are spoiled, but they're not being handed anything. They're working for it every day, learning that real security and freedom come from the sacrifices, choices, and discipline that build a life with purpose and integrity. And in the end, while it's hard work, it's the kind of work that will allow them to stand on their own two feet with pride, knowing they earned everything they have.

In essence, with this way of raising our kids, we do not desire or expect them to be "spoiled" in the traditional sense of indulgence and entitlement. Instead, we are dedicated to raising SPOILED kids—a new kind of "spoiled" that stands for *Savers, Producers, Owners, Investors, Leaders, Entrepreneurs,* and *Disciplined.* These are the attributes that we believe will equip our children to thrive, make meaningful contributions, and leave a legacy that reaches far beyond our lifetime. We're not aiming to hand them a life on a silver platter; rather, we're giving them the tools, the mindset, and the skills to build, nurture, and grow their own paths to success.

In this book, we'll share our approach for raising children who are financially savvy, capable of creating opportunities, and resilient in the face of challenges. We'll walk you through practical strategies for instilling the values of saving, producing, owning, investing, leading, and disciplined living in your children. Each chapter will delve into actionable ways to cultivate a mindset of self-sufficiency, entrepreneurship, and community responsibility, empowering you to build a wealth-generating legacy that not only benefits your children but also plants seeds for generations to come.

Through real-life examples, step-by-step practices, and insights drawn from our own journey, we'll show you how you, too, can raise *SPOILED* kids who redefine what it means to be "rich"—not just in terms of material wealth but in character, purpose, and impact. This book is more than just a parenting guide; it's a blueprint for creating a legacy that reflects your values and endures long after you're gone.

Whether you're a new parent or someone with older kids looking to instill these principles, or teacher, administrator, aunt, uncle, or community worker, you'll find the tools, encouragement, and inspiration needed to set your children on a path toward lasting success and meaningful contribution.

SET AN INTENTION FOR THIS BOOK

BEFORE YOU DIVE IN, PAUSE AND SET AN INTENTION FOR YOUR JOURNEY WITH THIS BOOK. INTENTION IS MORE THAN A GOAL — IT'S THE COMPASS THAT WILL GUIDE HOW YOU READ, APPLY, AND LIVE OUT THE PRINCIPLES OF THE SPOILED MINDSET.

THIS BOOK IS NOT JUST INFORMATION — IT'S TRANSFORMATION. EACH CHAPTER IS DESIGNED TO CHALLENGE HOW YOU THINK ABOUT MONEY, FAMILY, AND LEGACY. BUT THE IMPACT DEPENDS ON WHAT YOU BRING TO IT.

USE THE PROMPTS BELOW TO SET A POWERFUL INTENTION FOR HOW YOU WILL ENGAGE WITH THIS BOOK AND APPLY ITS LESSONS. BE HONEST, BE SPECIFIC, AND WRITE AS IF YOU'RE PLANTING THE SEEDS FOR THE FUTURE YOU WANT TO GROW.

MY INTENTION STATEMENT:

I INTEND TO

_____

I COMMIT TO

_____

I WANT MY KIDS/FAMILY/STUDENTS TO LEARN

_____

BY THE END OF THIS BOOK, I HOPE WE WILL

_____

TAKE A MOMENT TO READ YOUR WORDS OUT LOUD. REVISIT THEM OFTEN AS YOU MOVE THROUGH THESE PAGES — THEY WILL SERVE AS BOTH YOUR FOUNDATION AND YOUR FUEL.

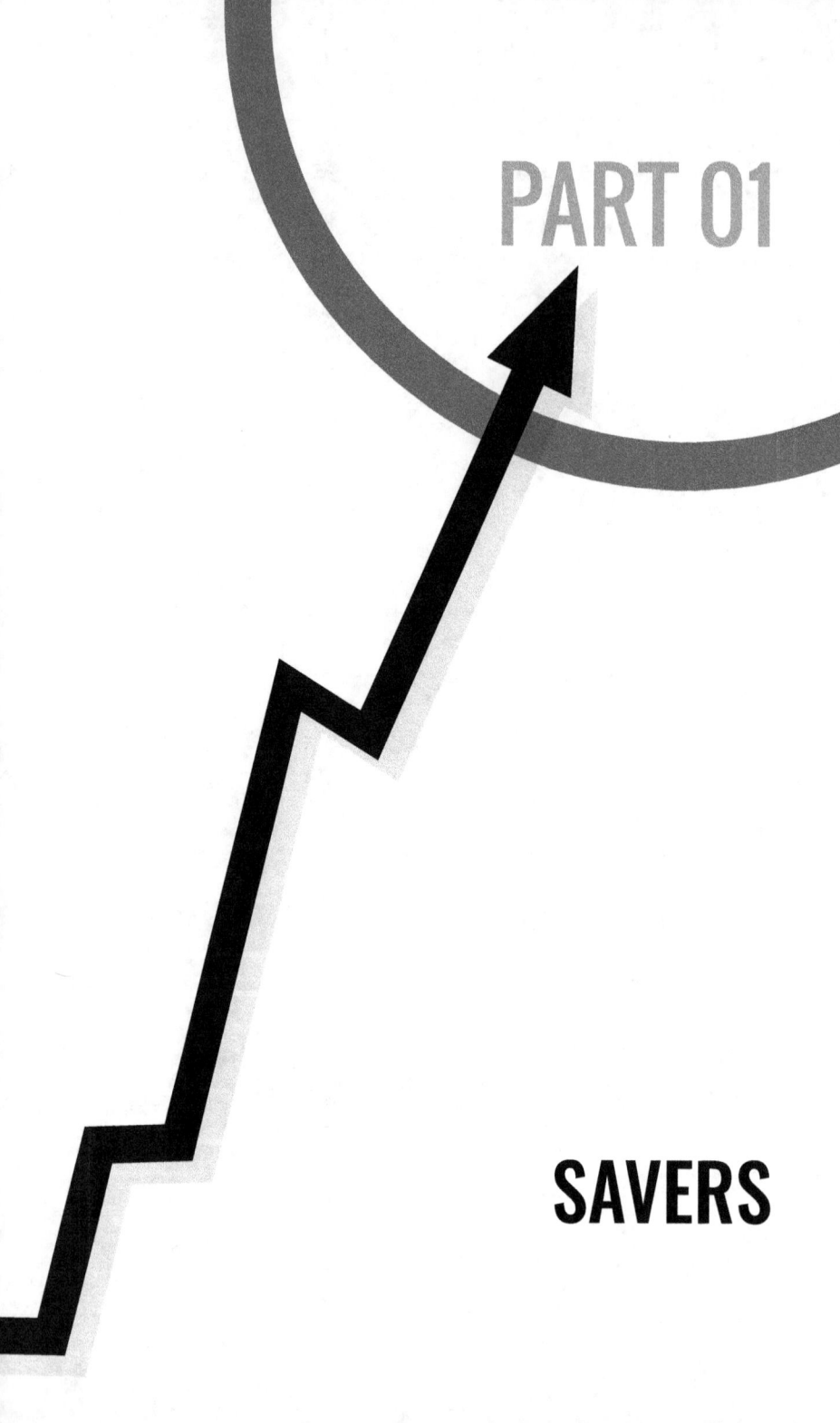

PART 01

SAVERS

Money was a touchy subject early in our marriage. We came from different backgrounds, each with our own beliefs, habits, and emotions tied to money, and it became clear very quickly that our ideas around savings, spending, and investing weren't aligned. Our contrasting perspectives caused a lot of friction—sometimes leading to heated arguments. One of us saw money as a necessary layer of security, something to be held onto and saved for rainy days, emergencies, and big future plans. In this view, every dollar in savings was like a shield against the unknown, providing stability and peace of mind.

The other, however, viewed money differently. They saw it as a tool meant to be used—a resource that existed to improve our quality of life right now. After all, what was the point of earning it if we weren't going to spend it on things that enriched our lives? This person believed that the more you earned, the more you "deserved"—a better car, designer clothes, a more spacious house. If you worked hard, then the reward should be tangible, not just sitting in a savings account. To them, savings felt more like a restriction than a pathway to freedom.

On top of these differing beliefs, we struggled with tracking our finances. One of us found budgeting and money management tedious and avoided tracking expenses altogether. Sometimes, money would go out, and we wouldn't even know where it had gone. Not actively managing our spending, saving, or even income sources created stress, uncertainty, and a feeling of helplessness. We both knew that something had to change, but we weren't sure where to begin. These different beliefs, paired with a lack of financial planning, made us feel out of control and anxious about the future.

Through trial and error, and after experiencing several financial setbacks that forced us to take a hard look at our finances, we began to educate ourselves. We started with the basics—learning what it meant to save, how to budget, and how to establish a more intentional approach to money. But beyond just the "how," we began exploring the psychology associated with money, realizing that it was not simply about the dollars and cents. It was about our relationship with money and how our pasts, upbringing, and values influenced the way we thought about it.

One of the most eye-opening moments came when we each dug into our own financial "scripts"—the unspoken beliefs about money that we'd unconsciously absorbed over the years. We learned that one of us grew up with a scarcity mindset, seeing money as something that could disappear at any moment, and so it had to be protected. The other had grown up with a mentality that emphasized the enjoyment of money, influenced by the idea that life was meant to be lived to the fullest without fear of running out. These beliefs weren't right or wrong—they were just different. Recognizing these influences allowed us to start working as a team to reframe our thinking and find a middle ground.

Together, we learned that saving wasn't about depriving ourselves or living in fear, but about building a foundation for future freedom and opportunities. We established a savings plan that worked for both of us, setting short-term and long-term goals that balanced security and enjoyment. We created an emergency fund, started contributing to retirement, and developed a habit of putting aside a portion of every paycheck for savings before spending on anything else. We even created separate accounts for "fun money" so that we could each enjoy guilt-free spending without jeopardizing our financial goals.

This journey taught us a lot about the goal of money and, fundamentally, what money actually is. Money isn't a measure of worth or happiness, but a tool—a resource that allows us to live out our values, achieve our goals, and make an impact. It's also a mindset. Today, we see savings not as a limitation but as a source of freedom, a way to build a life where we can take risks, seize opportunities, and weather life's inevitable storms without panic or worry.

This shift in our relationship with money not only brought us closer but also gave us a roadmap for teaching our children. By instilling in them the value of saving, we hope they'll grow up with a healthier perspective on money—one that embraces both the importance of planning for the future and the joy of experiencing life in the present. We've come to understand that building wealth isn't just about financial stability; it's about giving our family the freedom to live, grow, and give back to the world in meaningful ways.

In this section, we'll dive deeper into strategies for Saving for SPOILED Kids that aren't just practical but also achievable for any family. We'll explore how to build a healthy savings mindset, create effective savings habits, and avoid common pitfalls. Saving isn't about scarcity; it's about security, resilience, and creating a life where your financial resources align with your goals and values.

SAVERS 1.1:

What is Money?

It is important to understand that money, at its core, is only a symbol. It's a representation, a stand-in for value, but it is not the value itself. Money holds no inherent worth, it's completely neutral; its only power lies in the meaning, energy, and intention we place upon it. We tend to look at a bank balance or a paycheck and assign it a direct correlation to security, freedom, or status. But in reality, money is simply a tool—a medium that allows us to exchange time, skills, goods, and services within the world around us. It's a representation of our hard work, creativity, and, sometimes, sacrifice. Yet it doesn't define who we are or the quality of our lives.

When we begin to view money as a symbol rather than a source of value, our relationship with it can transform. Instead of seeing it as the ultimate goal or end, we recognize it as a means to other ends—such as stability, opportunity, generosity, and peace of mind. Money becomes less about acquiring things and more about creating a life that aligns with our values and purpose. This shift allows us to make financial decisions based not solely on the numbers, but on how those numbers will impact the lives we wish to lead.

To create the SPOILED child you must assist them in changing their thinking. Help them embrace the concept that money is only a tool, a symbol of value, rather than a measure of their worth or happiness. When they learn this, they grow up equipped with a healthy relationship with money, seeing it as a resource to support their goals and dreams rather than a source of stress or comparison. By understanding money's symbolic nature, the SPOILED child develops the wisdom to focus on things that hold true and lasting value—relationships, experiences, learning opportunities, physical and mental health, and steadfast values that guide them through life.

When asking a child, "What do you want to be when you grow up?," we usually get a fantastic, important, grand dream that will net them as much money as they can think of that will help them live a rich and secure life. We should support their goals no doubt, but more importantly, we should be promoting and instilling practical principles that help them become better humans rather than simply going after what they perceive will capture the most capital.

This perspective encourages children to prioritize genuine human connections and cherish experiences over material possessions. They learn that while money can facilitate comfort, it cannot replace the deep satisfaction that comes from meaningful friendships, time spent with loved ones, or giving back to their communities. They also begin to appreciate opportunities for personal and intellectual growth, viewing education, travel, and exploration as ways to expand their understanding of the world, rather than merely ways to accumulate wealth.

By instilling this mindset, you're also helping them appreciate the importance of physical and mental health. They come to understand that true wealth includes a healthy body, a resilient mind, and an ability to weather life's challenges with strength and optimism—no matter how much money they have at any given time. Rather than constantly seeking external validation or material status, they grow up grounded in their self-worth and sense of purpose.

When the SPOILED child views money as a tool rather than a trophy, they can better identify and commit to their core values—like integrity, empathy, and gratitude. These immovable principles guide their decisions and actions, shaping them into individuals who contribute positively to the world. They grow to understand that money, in its best use, is a vehicle for living out these values: whether it's used to support family, help those in need, invest in education, or create opportunities for others. In teaching your children to see money as a tool, you give them a foundation of resilience, perspective, and purpose that will serve them throughout their lives, allowing them to lead fulfilling lives centered on what truly matters.

By embracing money as a symbol, we also open ourselves to more sustainable wealth-building practices. We stop measuring success solely by dollar signs and start looking at our lives in terms of meaningful experiences, personal growth, and the legacy we leave behind. We start to understand that while money can help buy comfort or security, it cannot buy happiness, fulfillment, or a sense of purpose. Such qualities are cultivated from within, shaped by our choices, relationships, and contributions. Recognizing money as a symbol allows us to put it in its proper place—a valuable tool, but not the entirety of value itself.

SAVERS 1.2:

Building a Savers Mindset

When we instill a savings mindset, we help our children appreciate the rewards of discipline. They learn to wait, to work toward a goal, and to feel the accomplishment that comes from achieving something they've genuinely earned. This not only strengthens their financial foundation but also helps them resist the pressures of the "right now" culture and build a life that values stability and thoughtful decision-making. In a world driven by immediacy, teaching the value of saving is a gift—a skill that will help them navigate both the present and future with confidence and resilience.

Building a healthy saver's mindset oes beyond merely creating a habit of setting aside money. It's about cultivating a fundamental shift in how people view, value, and interact with money—essentially a paradigm shift from seeing money as something to be spent impulsively to viewing it as a tool for long-term stability and opportunity. This shift begins with encouraging a *growth mindset,* which is the belief that abilities and intelligence can be developed through effort, learning, and persistence. When children understand that financial literacy and responsibility are skills they can build and improve upon, they're more motivated to embrace disciplined saving and mindful spending as achievable goals, rather than restrictive practices.

In this journey, *critical thinking* plays a central role. Teaching children to analyze and question their choices empowers them to assess their spending habits, ask questions about needs versus wants, and think through the long-term impacts of their financial decisions. It encourages them to pause and weigh their options rather than acting on impulse. For instance, rather than buying the latest gadget, they can critically assess whether this purchase aligns with their larger financial goals, such as saving for a significant experience or investment.

Encouraging *divergent thinking* in this context helps children view saving as a creative, flexible process rather than a rigid rule. They learn to explore various ways to achieve their financial goals—perhaps by finding alternative sources of income, seeking out deals, or even negotiating a better price. Divergent thinking allows them to see saving as an adaptable and innovative part of their life, not just an obligatory task. When children can think creatively about how they allocate their money, they're more likely to stay engaged with the process and find satisfaction in achieving their goals.

Together, these concepts build a mindset where saving is less about restriction and more about empowerment. Once you have this mindset yourself, you can help your children see saving as a tool that opens doors to new opportunities. They can then experience the satisfaction of working toward something meaningful, whether it's a family trip, a business venture, or an educational fund. This foundation is about more than accumulating money; it's about developing a mindset that prioritizes long-term goals, thoughtful planning, and adaptability in the face of challenges. In cultivating this saver's mindset, they're also learning the essential life skills of patience, self-discipline, and strategic thinking, all of which will serve them well into adulthood.

In essence, building a healthy saver's mindset in a SPOILED child involves a combination of paradigm shifts, creative problem-solving, and a commitment to personal growth, equipping them to handle financial decisions with confidence, creativity, and purpose.

SAVERS 1.3:

Name Your Money

Teaching children to develop a Savers mindset begins with understanding the "Why." When children know the purpose behind saving, it becomes easier for them to resist impulsive spending, pause and think about needs versus wants, and steer clear of the debt traps that come with "buy now, pay later" attitudes. Knowing the "Why" grounds them in a greater purpose and encourages them to think about their future, rather than just immediate gratification.

One of the best ways to solidify this mindset is by *Naming Your Money*. This practice brings saving from the abstract into a tangible reality, giving each dollar a specific meaning and purpose. In our family, each savings account is named according to the goal it's connected to. The names we choose are simple and specific—like "Thailand Trip," "Honda in Cash," "South Africa," "Investment Fund," "Down Payment for Home," "Anniversary," and "Emergency Fund." By attaching real names to savings goals, each dollar feels like it belongs to something tangible, making it more meaningful and less tempting to spend. When we look at these names, they remind us of our purpose, and it becomes easier to resist the impulse to buy something fleeting.

Named funds also strengthen commitment. When we feel the urge to overspend or add something extra to our online cart, seeing labels such as "Thailand Trip" or "New Kitchen" gives us a reason to pause. We're reminded of the bigger picture and feel motivated to stay the course. This practice has helped our family maintain focus, stay disciplined, and experience the satisfaction of working toward something valuable.

Each of these names can be associated with short-term, medium-term, and long-term goals. A short-term goal typically involves something we plan to purchase within the next one month to two years. A medium-term goal covers items we aim to save for and purchase within two to five years. A long-term goal, on the other hand, is set for something we expect to buy or invest in five years or more down the road. For example:

Short-term goals: like "New Shoes" or "Laptop" can help children learn to prioritize and save for items they'll enjoy in the near future.

Medium-term goals: like "Fall Break in Brazil" or "Grand Canyon with Grandparents" show them the rewards of patience and planning.

Long-term goals: like "Education Fund" or "Investment Property" teach them about saving for future opportunities, giving them a sense of responsibility and anticipation.

It is important to have family meetings, both formal and informal, to regularly talk about these named accounts and share updates on progress toward these goals. For example, at the store, your child may ask you to buy a particular item that is outside the budget or more of a want that you believe the child can go without. Instead of saying, "No.... Because I said so," type of response, you could instead refer to one of the goals by name to remind them to stay focused on the path they've agreed to travel rather than spend the money dedicated to the goal. In turn, children learn that saving is a part of everyday life, not just something you do when you have extra money.

They see their savings grow and understand the real-world applications of their efforts, recognize the sacrifices, and strengthen their financial mindset. In this way, saving becomes an intentional, rewarding journey that's rooted in real-life goals.

SAVERS 1.4:

Break Goals Down

When we first envisioned the larger goals for our family, they felt almost out of reach. We weren't entirely sure *how* we would accomplish them, and there were moments when we felt a mix of excitement and anxiety. We believe that your dreams should be ambitious—big enough to stretch your abilities and inspire growth. If a goal is easily attainable, it might mean you're not challenging yourself enough to rise to your full potential. Big goals push you into unfamiliar territory, where growth takes place—an essential part of achieving meaningful success.

In setting goals that truly matter, we've found that understanding the *"why"* behind them is fundamental. Once we know "why" we're working toward something, it naturally leads us to ask, "'what' do we need to achieve this?" Then, once the 'what' is defined, we can focus on the 'how'—the steps to bring it to life.

For our family, this approach helps transform vague dreams into real, achievable goals. For example, if our *Why* is to create lasting memories and broaden our family's understanding of the world, our *What* becomes something tangible, like planning a trip to a new country. The *How* then becomes the practical steps we need to take to make it happen: saving a specific amount each month, budgeting our current expenses, and perhaps even setting up a separate "Vacation Fund," often named for the thing or place we envision going or doing. This helps to keep us motivated and on track.

With larger goals that feel intimidating, this progression from *Why* to *What* to *How* makes the journey feel clear and intentional. The *Why* keeps us inspired; it's the purpose that gives our efforts meaning. The *What* focuses our attention on the specific outcome we want, so we know exactly where we're headed. And the *How* brings it down to earth, breaking it into actionable steps that guide us along the way.

This process also helps our children grasp the purpose behind their efforts. When they understand *why* saving is important, they are more invested in the process. They see that they're not just setting aside money but are part of a bigger family goal, whether it's a memorable experience, a long-term investment, or an act of financial security. By showing them the *What* and guiding them through the *How*, we're teaching them to approach goals methodically and with purpose, turning dreams into a structured plan they can execute step by step.

For example, let's say you're saving for a family trip abroad or a down payment on a home. Instead of focusing on the entire amount you'll need, create a plan to set aside a specific amount each month. This makes the process feel more achievable and allows you to track your progress along the way. Each smaller milestone you reach provides a boost of motivation and a reminder that you're steadily moving closer to the ultimate goal. We can proudly remember our daughters coming home with a dollar or some coins in hand and saying, "This," excitedly holding up their currency, "belongs to Puerto Rico!" They would then proceed to place it in a jar we've set aside for such treasures to reside before depositing it into our savings account.

When goals are far off in the distance, it's easy to feel discouraged or lose sight of them amidst day-to-day responsibilities. But when you have smaller, measurable steps in place, you're regularly reminded of your progress, and it's easier to stay excited and motivated about your journey. Each saved dollar, each accomplished step, brings you one move closer to that larger vision, creating a steady path that turns a seemingly unreachable dream into a series of small, achievable actions.

In this way, our approach to savings and larger goals is more than just a financial plan; it's a life philosophy. It teaches resilience, patience, and strategic thinking.

When we keep our *Why*, *What*, and *How* in focus, even the most ambitious goals feel achievable. And that's a mindset we hope our children will carry with them throughout their lives.

SAVERS 1.5:

Understand Your Spending Habits

The first few years of our marriage were frustrating to say the least. When it came to our money, we constantly fought about our differing philosophies regarding money. We truly didn't understand each other's point of view and pointed the finger at each other for who was the one "messing up" our finances. What should have been a happy time getting to know one another and amalgamating our thoughts, feelings, beliefs, and experiences, was nothing short of, what seemed like, all out war. The solution, which didn't work at all, was to separate our finances into separate accounts, paying separate bills, earning separate monies. This quickly became "*my* money," "that was *your* bill," "*my* credit card," "*you* didn't pay this or why should *I* pay *your* bill?" We rationalized that this was the best way to preserve and "respect" our differing philosophies and triggers about money, but it just led to more feelings of distrust and frustration that we couldn't seem to shake. The worst part of it: our girls witnessed more of our losses than our wins. What we didn't realize at the time was that we were just normalizing dysfunctional financial behaviors.

We tend to get our beliefs, rituals, attitudes, values, and experiences first from our parents or caregivers when we ourselves were children. Generally, how your parents handled, valued, or talked about money is often the foundational education you receive about it. If one parent was gambling their paycheck away every two weeks, you may grow up with a sense that you should squirrel away money from your partner to "protect" it from their habit. Your grandmother may say something like, "Don't ever depend on no one for nothing. Make sure you have a secret account just in case." You may have witnessed your father miserly pinching every penny within your household, but abundantly generous to strangers. As an adult you may now be known as a giver while your immediate family gets less. Because of this, your childhood exposure to money can become your financial philosophy that triggers your habits as adults.

In time, we began to mature, gradually developing a deeper self-awareness about our relationship with money. We started by examining the influences that shaped our early perceptions—our individual upbringings, the financial habits modeled by our parents, and even the cultural messages we absorbed. This process revealed that, in many ways, we had been spending, saving, and managing money almost on autopilot, echoing the patterns and habits we'd picked up as children. These behaviors felt natural, but we came to realize they were less intentional choices and more unconscious remnants of our past.

It took some personal growth, reflection, and honesty with each other to accept that we didn't have to be limited by these ingrained ideas. We discovered it was not only okay but necessary to pull out the best parts of our financial upbringing—those practices that aligned with the life we envisioned—and let go of the parts that weren't serving us. For example, where one of us held on to the idea that spending could equate to joy, we reframed that value into spending purposefully on experiences rather than material possessions. And where saving for security had led to reluctance around healthy investments, we shifted that perspective to make smart investments part of our family's foundation for security.

This journey also helped us see that our parents' financial perspectives and the experiences that shaped them—though valuable—might not fully support the life we wanted to build. The world was different for us, and it was okay to adapt to meet our needs. Once we began sharing these realizations, we were able to define our *own* values around money—values that would guide our financial decisions as a couple and as parents. We spoke openly about what was important to each of us and clarified the role we wanted money to play in our lives. These conversations formed the basis of a financial plan that supported not only our marriage but also the legacy we hoped to pass down to our children and future generations.

In essence, our journey was about redefining financial values to fit the family we were creating, rather than the families we came from. We realized that by taking the time to design a financial framework centered on our unique goals and shared values, we could give our children a new foundation—a balanced, forward-thinking approach to money that would benefit them in the years and generations to come.

SAVERS 1.6:

Practice Delayed Gratification

In today's world, we live in a "right now" culture. Nearly anything we want is available instantly, creating a sense of immediacy that permeates almost every aspect of life. This culture of instant gratification makes it challenging for anyone—especially young people—to grasp the importance of patience, planning, and saving for the future.

We see this in the simplest daily transactions. Gone are the days of driving to an ATM or a bank branch to withdraw cash before making a purchase. Today, we can double-tap the side of a smartphone to "tap" a point-of-sale machine, paying instantly for our goods or services without ever reaching for a wallet. Need to send money to a friend overseas? With just a few swipes, funds arrive in their account within seconds. The immediacy extends beyond finances, too. Entertainment, once something we anticipated with excitement, is now at our fingertips 24/7. No longer do we wait for our favorite TV show to air weekly. With streaming, we can watch entire seasons in one sitting, no commercials or waiting required.

Social interaction has also been redefined by

immediacy. Where we once needed to wait until the next day at school to catch up with friends, or call them on the phone when it was free, now we can interact with hundreds of people around the world through social media apps, messaging, and video calls. With endless entertainment and instant social connections available at all times, the act of waiting has become unfamiliar, even obsolete.

This "right now" culture, while convenient, can undermine the patience and discipline needed to build financial stability. Saving money becomes difficult when we're accustomed to having our desires fulfilled immediately. It's easy to fall into the trap of thinking, *Why wait to save up for something when we can have it now?* But that mindset often leads to impulsive spending and an aversion to delay gratification—two things that are at odds with the concept of savings.

Teaching children about saving in a world where "right now" is the norm requires an intentional approach. They need to understand that while instant access is enticing, some of the best things in life come from patience, persistence, and planning. Encourage your children to use the 24-Hour Rule: this is when they wait a day before making non-essential purchases. This gives them time to think and helps them make intentional decisions rather than impulsive ones. Help them recognize that saving requires small sacrifices and can help prioritize future rewards over instant satisfaction.

By learning to delay gratification, they develop a mindset that prioritizes long-term goals over short-term pleasures. Saving becomes a powerful habit, allowing them to build a foundation that provides security, opportunities, freedom to pursue larger dreams, and keeps them away from the debilitating constraints of debt. As Nathan W. Morris put it, "Every time you borrow money, you're robbing your future self." Teach your children to be patient, delay the gratification of immediate pleasures, and to not steal from their future by paying in the present for something bought in the past.

Savers 1.7:

Reward Small Wins

In our family, we encourage our daughters to approach life with a winning mindset. We tell them often: *You were born to win.* Winning is not just an outcome but a birthright, something they are designed to do. We emphasize that winning in life comes from a series of wins that build on each other over time—the big wins that will shape their future are made possible by winning year after year, month after month, and day after day.

To make this idea tangible, we created a family "Wins Chart" where each family member proudly records their daily achievements, their *wins*. Our chart tracks seven categories of daily wins: *Academic, Business, Family, Financial, Mental, Physical,* and *Spiritual.* Each day, no matter how big or small the accomplishment is, everyone takes a moment to record something they achieved in each area. These could be as simple as completing a challenging homework assignment, reaching a small savings goal, getting up early to work out, helping someone in need, or taking time for self-reflection. This daily acknowledgment creates a positive loop of achievement, reinforcing the mindset that each small victory contributes to a larger picture.

We've made it a practice to hold regular family meetings where everyone shares their wins from the week. This isn't just about celebrating big milestones; it's about acknowledging every little step along the way. By doing this, we remind our daughters that small daily wins accumulate into the big ones, and this can outweigh the inevitable setbacks and challenges that come with any journey. Many people get stuck focusing on their losses or setbacks, fixated on the shadows rather than the light. Instead, we want our daughters to see that even setbacks can offer valuable lessons and lead to growth.

In addition to the Wins Chart we have up, we each keep a journal to record each one of their wins and reflect on them in detail. Through this practice, we teach our daughters to find gratitude in the journey, learning to celebrate each win and cultivate a mindset of abundance. When they appreciate their wins, they shift their focus away from what they lack and toward everything they already possess. They learn that success is not perfection; the forward motion is what truly matters.

We also celebrate milestones, large and small, to mark their progress toward their larger goals. For example, if one of our daughters reaches a specific savings target, we celebrate with a reward, not as an indulgence, but as positive reinforcement of their saving habits. And since we all can be extremely competitive, we have healthy (although sometimes hilariously intense) competitions to see who can accumulate the most wins in a month. The "wins" winner will get a predetermined prize we've voted on at the beginning of the month. The prizes have been diverse: each person contributes a favorite item of the winner; the winner can forgo chores for a week; the winner receives $1 per win, and more. This approach encourages consistency, showing them that progress, rather than perfection, is the real objective.

In essence, we teach them that a winning mindset is rooted in recognizing and celebrating every small step forward. Whether the victories are financial, academic, mental, or spiritual, they understand that the journey itself is a series of wins. When they can see every day as an opportunity to win, they become motivated, resilient, and confident, ready to take on whatever life throws at them.

SAVERS 1.8:

Visualize Your Financial Future

When working towards a specific goal, whether it's financial or personal, it's essential to have a clear and vivid picture of what that goal looks and feels like. This clarity not only helps you stay focused but also enables you to recognize when you've achieved your desired outcome and when you're still on your journey. Without a clear image, it becomes easy to be distracted or discouraged by the inevitable challenges that arise along the way.

When it comes to financial goals, one of the most powerful tools we use is visualization. It's important to help your children see their goals in as much detail as possible. Sit down with them, close their eyes, and guide them through the process of imagining what they want to achieve. Encourage them to describe the goal in vivid detail—how it looks, how it feels, and why it matters to them. This exercise helps create an emotional connection to their goals, making it more meaningful and easier to pursue.

Once they've articulated their vision, have them write it down. Research consistently shows that writing things down significantly enhances memory and commitment. Writing makes the goal more tangible, more real. It also serves as a constant reminder of the journey they're on, providing motivation during moments of doubt or distraction. The more vivid and specific the description, the stronger their resolve will be to stay the course.

In addition to writing down their goals, encourage them to create a vision board. A vision board is a visual representation of their dreams. By pinning images of their financial goals—whether it's a car, a home, a vacation, or even the concept of debt freedom—they're able to physically see what they are working toward. These boards act as powerful visual cues, reinforcing why they're saving and what they're working toward. The images serve as a daily reminder of their purpose and motivate them to take action.

Another effective tool is having them imagine their future selves. Help them picture the feelings of security, freedom, and peace of mind they will experience once they reach their financial goals. Ask them to visualize the life they will have when they are debt-free, financially independent, or able to make a large purchase without worry. By tapping into these positive feelings and experiences, they will create a deeper emotional connection to their savings journey, strengthening their motivation and perseverance.

Visualization helps keep their eyes on the prize, preventing distractions from steering them off course.

When the road gets tough, having a strong mental picture of the rewards will provide the necessary fuel to keep moving forward. Whether it's the feeling of buying a high priced item using cash instead of debt, or buying that first car with their own money, the vision of their future self can make all the difference in staying committed and achieving their goals.

Savers 1.9:

Financial Literacy

In your pursuit of raising a SPOILED Kid it is very important that you learn more about money. Financial literacy is the foundation of a successful, financially secure life. Make it a priority to expand your knowledge through books, podcasts, and online courses focused on saving, investing, and budgeting. Building this knowledge doesn't have to be a solo journey—engaging in these resources as a family can create a shared understanding and commitment to financial goals.

A powerful first step in any financial literacy journey is cultivating a practice of gratitude. Gratitude shifts our focus away from what we don't have and redirects it toward the abundance already present in our lives, making it easier to resist the urge to spend on non-essential items. Start by embracing this yourself and modeling it for your children, reinforcing the idea that true fulfillment often comes from valuing experiences, relationships, and personal growth rather than material possessions. When children learn to appreciate activities, connections, and moments, they naturally place less importance on accumulating "stuff." This mindset doesn't just reduce impulse spending; it enhances their lives by fostering a deeper sense of contentment, resilience, and genuine joy that goes beyond the fleeting satisfaction of new purchases. Practicing gratitude is, therefore, both a financial habit and a life skill that enriches in meaningful, lasting ways.

Consider visiting our website, www.MySPOILEDKids.com, to discover a range of resources designed to help your family succeed. Our interactive financial education course, for example, is a great tool for parents and children to learn the essentials together. Here, you'll find hands-on activities, discussions, and practical applications for mastering financial skills such as setting a budget, understanding compound interest, and creating savings goals as you and your children become certified SPOILED Kids! Learning about money as a family helps to establish a supportive, informed environment where financial habits are not only taught but modeled, reinforcing the journey toward a disciplined and financially empowered mindset.

An active pursuit of financial literacy is a lifelong skill. In an ever-changing global economy, there is always something to learn and grow in your knowledge of how finances operate. You not only equip yourself but also set an invaluable example for your children, fostering a culture of understanding and responsibility around money that will serve them throughout their lives.

SAVERS 1.10:

Understand Compound Interest

Understanding the power of saving early and consistently is one of the most valuable lessons in building wealth. When you save and invest even small amounts regularly, your money has time to grow exponentially, thanks to compound interest. Compound interest means that the returns you earn on your savings start generating their own returns, creating a snowball effect. Over time, the growth of your savings accelerates, allowing you to build wealth with relatively minimal ongoing effort.

For example, a small amount set aside each month can, over the years, grow into a substantial sum without requiring drastic lifestyle changes. The earlier you start, the more your money works for you, often doubling or tripling its value as it compounds. This not only leads to financial security but also creates a sense of confidence and freedom, knowing that your future is supported by years of thoughtful planning and consistent saving. Even if you can't save large amounts, the key is consistency—every contribution builds momentum. Through early and consistent saving, you develop financial resilience, giving you greater freedom to pursue passions, withstand setbacks, and provide security for yourself and your loved ones.

Try this exercise with your SPOILED Children: Ask them, "Would you rather receive $10,000 each day for thirty days or just a single penny that doubles each day for thirty days?" Most children—and many adults—might eagerly choose the $10,000 daily option, as it would provide an impressive total of $300,000 in just one month. Truly this is for most of us life changing money. However, this exercise reveals the surprising power of compound growth.

In the penny-doubling scenario, your child might be shocked to learn that by day thirty, that single penny grows to well over $10 million! This incredible leap happens due to the magic of compound interest, where each day's increase builds on the day before. If they continue doubling for just one more day, the total would exceed $20 million. Wow! How much more life-changing would this be? Managed correctly that could last for generations.

This powerful example highlights how even modest savings can grow to substantial amounts when time and compounding are on their side. It's an engaging way to show children that small, steady contributions—when saved consistently—can grow exponentially, far beyond what they might initially expect. Breaking down the process and discussing the math together reinforces the lesson, helping them understand how choosing patience and consistent saving today can create tremendous wealth and financial security over time.

This exercise not only teaches your SPOILED Child the numbers behind compounding but instills a mindset of patience and delayed gratification. Through this, they learn that the true rewards of saving and investing come not in the initial amount, but in how it grows over time, guiding them toward a disciplined and strategic approach to money management.

You can find great examples, fun worksheets, and our SPOILED Family Course on our website www.MySPOILEDKids.com.

SAVERS 1.11:

Create a Saver's Network

No one is truly alone. In fact, we're all part of a vast network of people, communities, and systems that rely on one another to keep life running efficiently and smoothly. When we feel isolated or think we must carry the weight of our goals alone, the world seems to grow bigger and more overwhelming, while we feel smaller and less capable. But when we allow others to support and collaborate with us, our world becomes smaller and more manageable, while we gain strength, confidence, and the perspective that our goals are achievable.

One powerful way to stay motivated is to join like-minded communities as part of your saver's network, which shares similar goals. surrounding yourself with others who share a saver's mindset can make all the difference. These communities offer a support system, with members sharing advice, tips, and encouragement that can help each of us reach our goals faster. Whether it's joining online groups on social media platforms, attending local financial literacy workshops, or becoming part of a financial club, being around others with a saver's mindset can make all the difference. This can lead to positive and valuable peer pressure for your SPOILED Kids to have healthy competitions, inspiration, and motivation to build their savings.

Incorporating the help of trusted friends or family members can be equally effective. When you express your goals aloud to people you trust, it helps solidify your commitment. These individuals become cheerleaders and accountability partners who remind you why you started and encourage you to keep going. Surrounding yourself with supportive voices is especially helpful during moments of doubt or temptation, offering a reminder that the journey is worth it.

In a community of like-minded people, you'll gain the wisdom of those who have already overcome similar challenges and can offer advice on avoiding pitfalls, maximizing savings, or investing wisely. Through shared experiences, your sense of isolation decreases, and suddenly your goals don't feel as daunting. Remember, building a healthy financial future is not something that has to be done alone; in fact, it can be much more fulfilling and effective when it's a shared journey.

We have links to some great online resources, social savers networks, and other ways to connect with SPOILED Families all around the world on our website www.MySPOILEDKids.com..

SAVERS 1.12:

Plan for Unexpected Expenses

To plan effectively for life's inevitable pitfalls and setbacks, developing a *preparedness mindset* is essential. Preparedness is more than just saving for a rainy day—it's a way of thinking that transforms fear of the unknown into confidence in your ability to handle it. It's the difference between reacting to life and proactively positioning yourself to navigate it. When we teach children this mindset early, we're not just preparing them for emergencies—we're equipping them with resilience, resourcefulness, and emotional stability for the rest of their lives.

For your SPOILED Kid, building an Emergency Fund is a powerful and practical first step. This simple concept lays the foundation for lifelong financial wisdom. It's not just about money—it's about discipline, foresight, and peace of mind. When a child understands *why* emergencies happen and *how* they can prepare for them, they begin to see unexpected events not as crises but as manageable challenges.

Start small. Set a goal together—maybe $50 or $100—and frame it as a "safety net" for life's surprises.

As they grow more consistent with saving, work toward a larger goal: enough to cover three to six months of their personal "expenses." While children usually don't have significant costs, you can simulate real-world budgeting by assigning age-appropriate responsibilities.

For example, if your teenager has a cell phone, have them contribute a small portion of the monthly bill. Then challenge them to save enough to cover six months of payments. If they care for a pet, encourage them to save for food or vet costs. These exercises make financial responsibility tangible and show that every choice has a cost.

Involving children in this process helps them *feel* the value of saving. They begin to understand that nothing is truly free—that the things they want and enjoy require care, planning, and sacrifice. This lesson cultivates a deeper appreciation for their possessions and the money it takes to sustain them. It also builds a healthy sense of ownership: they're no longer passive recipients of things but active stewards of their choices.

Having an emergency fund also offers an invaluable emotional benefit—peace of mind. Knowing they have a cushion against the unexpected reduces anxiety and prevents them from dipping into other savings meant for future goals. It teaches them that money can be a tool for security and empowerment, not just spending.

Ultimately, the purpose of building an emergency fund isn't just financial—it's foundational. It instills a mindset of preparedness that extends far beyond money. When your child learns to anticipate challenges rather than fear them, they develop resilience. When they learn to plan instead of panic, they build confidence. And when they learn to respond thoughtfully to the unexpected, they become independent.

By teaching your SPOILED Kid to save for the "what ifs," you're teaching them one of life's most powerful lessons: Preparation turns uncertainty into opportunity. And with that lesson, they'll walk into every challenge not with fear, but with faith in their ability to handle whatever comes next.

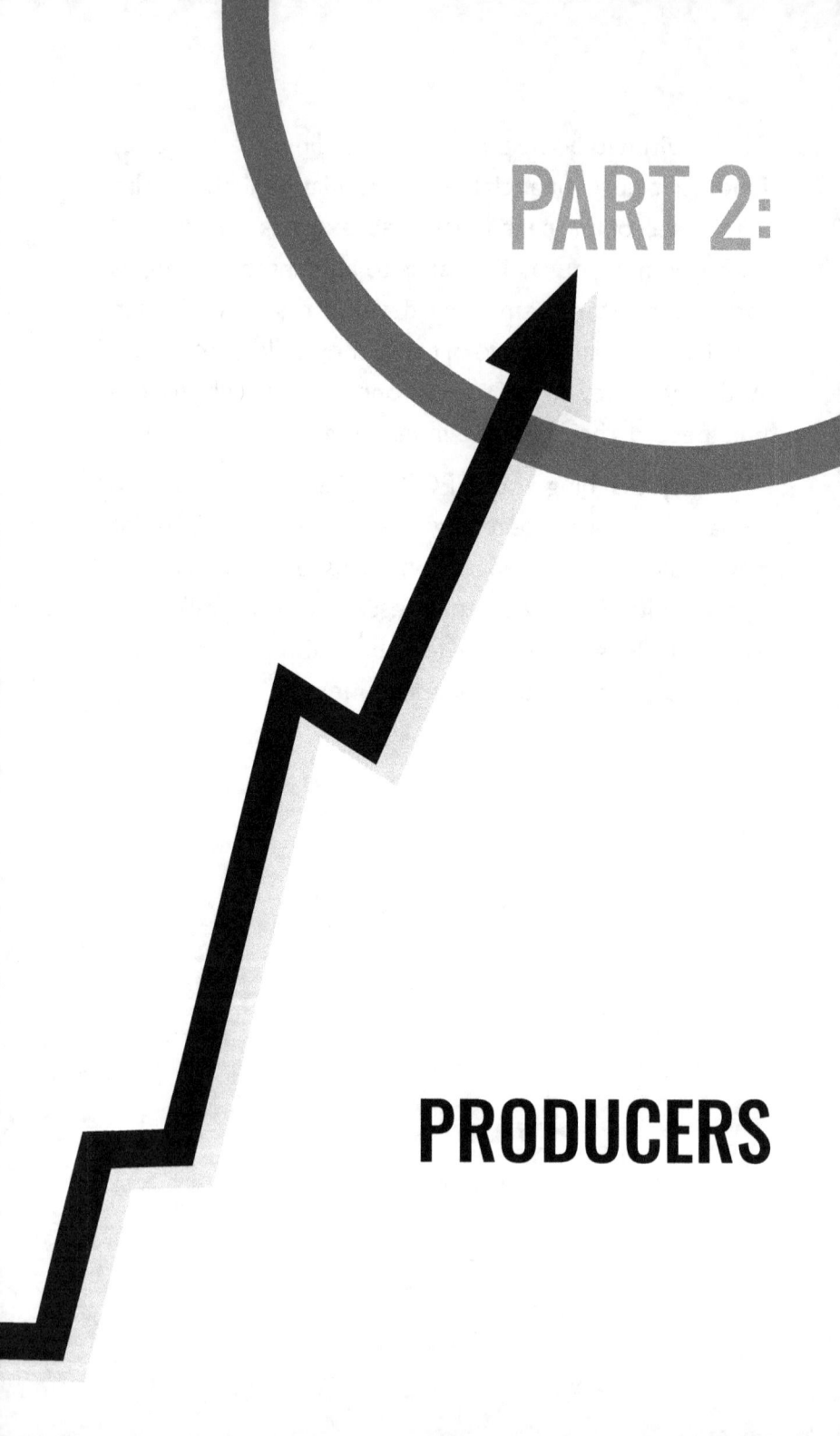
PART 2:
PRODUCERS

In economic terms, a producer is someone who creates and supplies goods or services, often combining resources such as labor, capital, knowledge, and materials to transform ideas into tangible outcomes. Producers are individuals who see opportunities where others see only limitations; they use their skills, knowledge, and hard work to bring new things into existence. They create value through innovation, craftsmanship, problem-solving, and dedication. In the simplest a sense, producers don't merely consume what's available—they create something unique, adding to the world around them.

When our family decided to live a lifestyle free from animal products, we soon learned just how challenging it could be to find products, restaurants, and social spaces that supported this choice. For example, traveling was a particular struggle. Airport options were limited to barely edible offerings like French fries cooked in the same oil as fried meat products or "vegan salads" that were simply stripped-down versions of regular salads, often leaving us with only lettuce and a slice of cucumber. This was a recurring theme, not just while traveling but also when dining out locally, attending social gatherings, or even family events. Our decision became a source of lighthearted jabs from family members, and the limited variety of options in our own city felt like an additional obstacle. Instead of feeling discouraged, however, this experience sparked something powerful in us: a deep resolve to create the change we wanted to see. Rather than complain, we would create.

Instead of passively accepting the lack of options, we saw an opportunity to innovate. We tapped into our entrepreneurial mindset and became producers, creating what was missing in our own lives and community. Our first step was researching vegan dishes we truly enjoyed. We didn't stop there, though—we went beyond the basics and used our family vacations as a way to explore and taste how different cultures around the world were embracing plant-based lifestyles. We found unforgettable vegan options in some of the most unexpected places, from vegan lasagna in Versailles, France, to vegan seafood in Cincinnati, Ohio. We discovered delicious vegan brownies on the beach in Ipanema, Brazil, and devoured creative vegan burgers in Atlanta. Across continents and cultures, we found inspiration and fresh ideas to bring home and make our own.

By the summer of 2019, we were ready to put this inspiration into action. With nothing more than a vision, a borrowed tent, and a grill from our brother-in-law, we founded Black Leaf Vegan. We started with a few reimagined American and international dishes like our Vegan Bacon Ranch Burger, Loaded Vegan Nachos, and Crabless Crabcakes. To our delight, our flavors and creativity quickly made a mark, turning Black Leaf Vegan into a local hit. What began as a tent soon transformed into a food trailer, which then became a food truck. In a historic moment for our family, we became the first vegan vendor at the Indiana State Fair, an event with a legacy of over 160 years.

We didn't stop there. We took the next step and acquired a bus, converting it into another food truck, and before long, we opened our first brick-and-mortar café in downtown Indianapolis. Just two years later, we opened a second location in Fishers, Indiana with many more envisioned in many places around the world. These accomplishments are deeply meaningful not just for us as parents, but also for our children, who have been involved in every part of the journey.

Our children didn't just watch this journey unfold; they actively participated. They are not only listed as owners on paper but are true partners in producing, running, and innovating within our business. From helping set up at food truck events to learning the art of customer service, they've been valuable contributors. Our children have learned to be creative problem-solvers, facing the real-world challenges of entrepreneurship and understanding what it means to be producers. They see firsthand the power of vision, hard work, and resilience in action. Involving them in this journey means more than building a family business; it's about building a legacy of creativity, self-reliance, and empowerment that they'll carry forward in their own lives, whatever they choose to create.

Through this journey, our family has come to embrace a shared philosophy: if something you need isn't available, create it. This is the essence of a producer's mindset, and we hope it will serve as an enduring lesson for our children as they face their own obstacles, pursue their own dreams, and build lives of purpose and contribution.

Our goal as parents is to nurture a mindset in our children that embraces this identity. We want them to see themselves as producers, capable of generating their own value and making meaningful contributions to their communities and the broader world. This is more than simply making things to sell. It's about fostering a mentality that sees beyond immediate consumption and instead focuses on the power and satisfaction of creation.

We encourage our children to dream big, using their imaginations to think up ways they can contribute, innovate, and create something that has personal and financial value. Whether through art, writing, coding, building, designing, or any other form of production, we want them to tap into their unique talents and interests. Teaching them that they are capable of producing value instills a sense of independence and confidence; it builds resilience and empowers them to become resourceful problem-solvers. As producers, they learn to take ownership of their ideas and translate them into reality, a skill that will benefit them throughout their lives.

In our family, we encourage this producer mindset by fostering ingenuity and exploration. If our children have a new interest or idea, we encourage them to pursue it, experiment, and make mistakes along the way. Sometimes, they'll create something small—a piece of art, a simple invention, or a written story. Other times, they'll work on bigger projects that might involve researching a market, identifying a need, and creating a solution for that need. We've made it clear that no idea is too big or too small to explore.

To further solidify this producer mentality, we've encouraged our children to think about monetizing their creations. From setting up small online stores for handmade items to helping with family business tasks, they're given chances to see the economic impact of their efforts. They learn not only about production but also about the value exchange that happens in a marketplace. We want them to understand that they can be active participants in the economy—contributors who have something valuable to offer, not just consumers relying on the labor of others.

A producer mentality also instills patience and discipline, teaching them to focus on the process as much as the result. Producing something worthwhile often takes time, commitment, and resilience. It's about seeing the steps involved, the small victories in each part of the process, and the satisfaction of putting in hard work to see an idea come to life. This experience builds discipline, as they learn that creativity alone isn't enough—they need to stick with projects even when challenges arise.

As parents, we support their growth as producers by helping them set goals, teaching them the skills they need to achieve those goals, and celebrating their accomplishments, big and small. We want our children to understand that being a producer isn't just about creating products or services; it's about becoming a creator in the larger sense—someone who has the courage and determination to bring something meaningful into existence, to solve problems, and to contribute something of value to the world. By embracing this role as producers, our children develop a sense of agency, purpose, and pride in their work that will shape their lives and futures.

Producers 2.1:

Cultivating a Producer's Mindset

Cultivating a producer's mindset is about fostering habits, attitudes, and values that emphasize creating over-consumption, generating solutions instead of waiting for them, and proactively shaping one's world rather than passively accepting it. For your SPOILED child, developing this mindset begins with valuing creativity and seeing themselves as capable of contributing something meaningful to the world.

Encourage your child to look at every obstacle as an opportunity in disguise and each problem as a spark for potential growth. When they experience setbacks, help them practice reframing these situations, so they start to ask, "What can I create to overcome this?" rather than "How can I get past this quickly?" This shift transforms challenges into exercises in creativity, resilience, and innovative thinking, essential qualities for any producer.

A producer's mindset also requires an understanding that every individual brings unique skills and perspectives that can add value to their communities and beyond. Show your child that they don't have to wait for ideal circumstances to produce something meaningful—they can start small and refine their abilities as they go. Help them realize that producing doesn't always mean creating a physical product; it can mean developing ideas, generating positive influence, or even building skills that they can share with others.

To reinforce this mindset, encourage projects where they can create solutions to real-world issues they care about, like a mini-business, a social media page with valuable content, or even household tasks where they can apply creativity. Involve them in conversations about identifying needs, brainstorming solutions, and designing goals that focus on creation over consumption. With this approach, your SPOILED child learns to see themselves not just as a consumer in the world but as a producer with the power to leave a unique mark, one imaginative project at a time.

PRODUCERS 2.2:

Encourage Creative Problem-Solving

SPOILED Producers view problems not as roadblocks but as opportunities to create, innovate, and think critically. To instill this mindset in your child, foster a habit of identifying challenges and exploring multiple ways to tackle them. This approach builds confidence and empowers them to view themselves as capable of shaping their environment rather than being shaped by it.

Start small by encouraging them to look around for things they wish were different or better, then help them brainstorm creative ways to improve those situations. For instance, if they're unsatisfied with their study space, encourage them to design an organized, inspiring corner using resources already available at home, like repurposed jars for pencils or decorative shelves they've built themselves. This practice helps them see that not everything needs to be bought; many solutions are within their reach, waiting for a bit of creative thinking and thoughtful execution.

If your child wants a unique costume for a school event, challenge them to design it from everyday items. Guide them to think through the process, like gathering materials, drawing sketches, and experimenting with fabrics, cardboard, or paints. By taking on this challenge, they learn about resourcefulness, adopt a hands-on approach to problem-solving and understand the satisfaction of bringing an idea to life from scratch.

This approach not only strengthens adaptability but also reinforces resilience, as they'll learn to handle setbacks or pivot their strategies as needed. They might find that some materials don't work as planned or that a design needs tweaking. Every small hurdle they overcome while building or creating something reinforces the lesson that solutions aren't always handed to us—they're crafted by those willing to try, learn, and keep improving.

Instilling a producer's mindset through creative problem-solving helps them grow into adults who see beyond surface-level challenges, instead recognizing the hidden potential for innovation. They learn to embrace curiosity, nurture their imagination, and develop a proactive attitude toward life's complexities—essential qualities for anyone looking to produce rather than passively consume.

PRODUCERS 2.3:

Goals Focused on Creation, Not Consumption

To become a SPOILED producer, it's important to set goals that focus on creating value and contributing, rather than just acquiring material items. This mindset encourages your child to view themselves as creators and problem-solvers. For example, instead of aspiring to own the latest toy or gadget, help them set a goal to develop a skill, create a product, or address a need—whether for the family or in the community. These goals could include developing a new skill, like coding or painting, making a unique art piece to sell online, or starting a small business such as selling homemade crafts or fresh produce at a local farmer's market.

Setting these kinds of goals shifts their thinking to become more proactive and purpose-driven. Goals like "I want to create my own blog where I can share my thoughts and connect with others" or "I want to save enough money to invest in starting a pet-sitting service" are meaningful because they focus on growth, initiative, and resourcefulness. By contrast, goals such as "I want to buy new clothes" or "I want the latest video game console" foster a mindset of consumption and often lack long-term fulfillment.

Encourage your child to create measurable, time-bound goals centered on production. Breaking these goals down into smaller, actionable steps—like setting aside time each week to learn a skill or tracking their savings progress—reinforces habits of discipline, patience, and resilience. It's also a great way for them to see tangible results, which builds confidence and gives them a sense of accomplishment.

Our middle child has an undeniable sweet tooth. Whether it's pastries, candy, bread, or anything else promising a sugar rush, she's drawn to it like a magnet. When she manages to get her hands on something sweet—whether by spending her own money or charming Grandma into buying it—she often turns into a self-proclaimed dessert critic. "This would be better if…" or "I like these, but I wish they would…" or even "I can taste the nutmeg, but cinnamon or Biscoff would give it the perfect balance."

Our response is usually something like, "Who is 'they'? And why should 'they' fix it when *you* can?" With a smile, she takes this challenge to heart and heads to the kitchen. She pulls out recipes, reads them carefully, and then puts her unique spin on each one. When she adds new ingredients or tweaks the process, we remind her, "That's not just an adjustment—it's a new recipe!" She writes it all down, experimenting with different creations, some of which delight us and others… well, let's just say they're part of the process.

We're always supportive yet honest with her. Over time, her collection of recipes began to grow, and one day, she asked, "Can I publish a cookbook of my treats?" Naturally, as a SPOILED Kid with a *Producer Mindset*, her instinct was to *create* what she wanted rather than simply consume it. Understanding that, instead of waiting and wanting something different, she has to be the change that she wanted to see.

Her desire to turn her sweet cravings into homemade creations is inspiring. She now rarely asks to buy snacks after school. Instead, she rushes home, dives into her ingredients, and gets to work. From rolling dough to brainstorming bold new flavor combinations, she's found a way to channel her creative spirit into something tangible and delicious. Even while everyone is sleeping, she wakes up early to try out something that was on her mind throughout the night. We—well, at least one of us—no longer gets bent out of shape when waking up to the kitchen in disarray. Flour all over the place gives us a sense of pride that she is learning, creating, and doing something that brings her joy. It's amazing to witness her turning her passion into productivity, reminding us all that true fulfillment often comes from creating what we crave not necessarily from what we consume. Don't worry, we are also getting her to fall just as much in love with cleaning as she does creating.

A SPOILED kid should always have ideas flowing, with a mindset geared toward possibility and improvement. Encourage brainstorming sessions where they can list out different ways to be productive or inventive, from designing DIY projects for the home to thinking of ways to reduce waste. This practice of thinking in terms of ideas rather than acquisitions teaches them that they don't need to wait for the world to give them something—they can create it themselves.

This approach to goal-setting not only inspires learning and independence but also teaches them that true wealth comes from what they contribute and create. It builds a foundation for lifelong skills like critical thinking, resourcefulness, and adaptability, equipping them to see the world not just as a place to consume, but as a canvas of endless opportunities to make a meaningful impact.

PRODUCERS 2.4:

New Skills Over Buying Solutions

SPOILED Producers thrive on continuous learning because they understand that knowledge and skills are the ultimate tools for creation. When confronted with a problem or a need, instead of immediately looking for a way to buy a solution, a producer's mindset actively seeks to acquire the skills necessary to address it. This mindset fosters a sense of independence and self-reliance, empowering individuals to be problem-solvers and creators in all areas of their lives.

For example, instead of simply purchasing a personalized picture frame, encourage your child or family member to learn how to make it. This small, hands-on project could involve learning basic woodworking, painting, or designing, which not only provides a meaningful outcome but also builds confidence in their ability to create. It teaches them that they have the power to craft their own solutions, rather than relying on external sources. The act of creating something from scratch, even something simple, helps to reinforce the value of learning and the satisfaction that comes from making something with your own hands.

Each new skill learned through these types of challenges is an investment in their future independence. Over time, these skills compound, allowing them to handle increasingly complex problems. As they continue to explore different learning opportunities, they begin to see that there is always a way to solve a problem, whether it's through developing technical skills, learning new trades, or honing artistic abilities.

For instance, learning how to code may open doors to building a website or even launching a small online business, while learning basic financial literacy and budgeting can empower them to manage a small business venture or personal savings with ease. On our website www.MySPOILEDKids.com, they can partake in many resources that inspire them to learn such as our SPOILED Family Course. As they acquire skills that serve both personal and professional goals, they develop an ever-growing toolkit of abilities that can be applied in countless areas of life, from managing a family budget to creating digital art or starting a side hustle. A SPOILED Kid's creative dream can lead to a hustle; hustle can lead to a business; and business can turn into a legacy for generations to come.

SPOILED Producers value continuous learning, which equips them to produce new things and refine existing skills. Encourage inquiry and exploration in a variety of topics that may be outside of one's usual comfort zone. A continuous learning mindset encourages curiosity and the persistence to keep going, even when things get challenging. It fosters resilience, as it teaches them that setbacks are part of the process of learning and growing. Each new lesson, whether it's practical or theoretical, can lead to more significant achievements down the road. Over time, this mindset can lay the foundation for a person to not just survive but thrive in a world where change is constant and opportunities for growth are endless.

By cultivating a love for learning and an appreciation for acquiring new skills, SPOILED Producers become empowered to take on any challenge that comes their way. They are no longer passive consumers; instead, they are active creators, constantly learning, evolving, and contributing to the world around them.

Producers 2.5:

Celebrate Process, Not Just Results

A SPOILED producer's mindset values the journey as much as the destination. This approach emphasizes the importance of recognizing and celebrating the effort, learning, and growth that occur throughout the process of creating something. Whether the end result is exactly what was envisioned or not, the focus remains on the journey—the steps taken, the lessons learned, and the resilience built along the way.

When a child, or anyone, puts in the effort to create—whether it's crafting a new recipe, painting a piece of art, writing a song, or launching an entrepreneurial venture—it's crucial to acknowledge and celebrate their commitment to the process. These are certainly wins. Acknowledging the work involved sends a powerful message that effort itself is valuable, regardless of the outcome. And without effort no win is even possible. For example, if a child tries their hand at making a cake from scratch and it doesn't come out perfectly, instead of focusing on the failure, you can celebrate the creativity and determination they displayed in making the attempt. Praising the effort reinforces the idea that the act of trying and learning is just as important—if not more so—than achieving perfection.

By celebrating the process of creating, people learn that growth happens through action, even when the outcome is imperfect. This mindset helps children—and adults—understand that failure is not something to fear, but a natural part of the learning process. It's through these imperfections that creativity and innovation can thrive. The willingness to take risks, to make mistakes, and to learn from those mistakes is what fosters true growth. For example, a child who fails at their first attempt at starting a small business will gain invaluable experience about what works, what doesn't, and how to pivot toward a better solution. This, in turn, helps to develop critical thinking, problem-solving skills, and perseverance.

When a producer's mindset is cultivated around the idea of valuing the journey, it builds a resilience that can weather challenges. Life, especially when it comes to creating, is filled with ups and downs. Things won't always go as planned, and projects may not always turn out perfectly. However, when the focus is on the growth and learning achieved along the way, these setbacks become less discouraging and more of an opportunity for development. This shift in perspective helps individuals build the emotional stamina and mental fortitude needed to keep going in the face of adversity.

Furthermore, celebrating the journey fosters a sense of pride in one's work. Whether the project is big or small, recognizing the effort and the incremental progress can boost confidence and reinforce the idea that every step forward counts. It helps to instill a deep sense of ownership over one's creations and accomplishments, encouraging people to continue to invest time and energy into future endeavors.

This mindset also makes the pursuit of goals more enjoyable. When the process itself is rewarding, there's less pressure to achieve perfection and more focus on the satisfaction that comes with progress. It creates a healthier relationship with productivity, where the drive to create is not solely motivated by an end goal, but by the satisfaction of the work itself. Let us be clear, we are not talking about the celebration of mediocrity, but the valiant mindset that puts forth one's best effort in pursuit of a meaningful goal.

When one of our daughters joined the track team, she took her training seriously. Every morning, she woke up early to stretch, complete her exercises, and attend practices, each day preparing herself for the upcoming races. In her first race, she finished second to last, with a time of five minutes and forty-three seconds—certainly not the result she had hoped for. Feeling defeated, she ran to us with tears in her eyes, whispering, "I lost, I can't believe I lost." She collapsed into our arms, and we held her tight.

This moment became a learning opportunity about resilience and the SPOILED Producer mindset, which values hard work, persistence, and the growth process. Looking into her eyes, we reassured her, "No, honey, you didn't lose—you just haven't won yet." This perspective shift rekindled her resolve. Determined to improve, she redoubled her efforts, showing up with even more grit for the next race. This time, she finished fifth. The difference was remarkable. Instead of tears of defeat, she was brimming with joy and ran over to us with a wide smile, shouting, "I won! I won!"

Her time improved from 5:43 to 5:31—an incredible leap. We celebrated with her, affirming, "Yes, you did! You most certainly did win." In that moment, she learned a critical lesson: winning isn't about coming in first against others; it's about achieving a personal best and embracing the journey toward improvement. Her goal for the season shifted to consistently improving her own performance, focusing on beating her own time rather than simply securing first place.

Had her only measure of success been to rank first, she might have missed the most important lesson about resilience and growth. Imagine if she had somehow placed first in her second race but with a slower time, say 5:53. She wouldn't have pushed herself harder the next time or understood the strength found in persistent effort. The SPOILED Producer mindset emphasizes that true success is measured not by a trophy but by the steady, dedicated commitment to personal improvement and hard work—a lesson far more valuable than any medal. In her last race of the season, she beat her best time with 4:02, a proud parent moment and a great achievement for our child.

Ultimately, a SPOILED producer's mindset builds a strong, resilient character that is not easily discouraged by setbacks or failures. By embracing the journey, learning from challenges, and celebrating the effort, individuals develop a deep sense of satisfaction and accomplishment that is rooted in their growth. This mindset encourages them to take on challenges, learn new skills, and create with confidence, knowing that each step forward is an important part of their personal and professional evolution.

PRODUCERS 2.6:

Encourage Experimentation and Risk-Taking

SPOILED Producers are often characterized by their openness to new experiences and their willingness to take calculated risks. This quality sets them apart, as they view unfamiliar challenges not with hesitation but with excitement and curiosity. Encouraging children—and yourself—to embrace this mindset means cultivating a habit of experimenting with ideas, even when the outcome is uncertain. By fostering this spirit of exploration, you help build confidence and resilience, two essential qualities for success in any venture.

Encourage this exploratory mindset in small, everyday ways. For instance, trying a new recipe can teach adaptability in the kitchen, sparking creativity as you work through unexpected issues with ingredients or technique. Similarly, launching a small project, like creating handmade items to sell at a local market or testing out a new idea for a business, can provide hands-on experience with problem-solving, planning, and overcoming challenges. Traveling to a new country, if possible, or even exploring new neighborhoods or cultures locally, allows for the expansion of perspectives and teaches adaptability in unfamiliar environments. Each of these experiences helps build resourcefulness, broadens thinking, and opens up pathways for more innovative ideas.

In the world of entrepreneurship or any field requiring creativity, risk-taking becomes essential for progress. Testing out a new product or concept, even on a small scale, helps develop important skills like research, strategy, and planning. These skills translate to other areas of life and reinforce the idea that failure isn't something to avoid but rather a natural part of growth. When ideas don't work out as planned, they become stepping stones for refinement and improvement, creating an opportunity to learn and strengthen the approach for the next attempt.

This approach to trying new things is rooted in a mindset of curiosity, which is the bedrock of learning and growth. Curiosity encourages children and adults alike to question how things work, explore possibilities, and engage actively with the world around them. When mistakes happen—and they will—they serve as valuable lessons. Encourage a habit of reflection after each new experience, whether it goes well or not, so you can analyze what worked, what didn't, and how to approach the task differently next time. This reflective process helps individuals develop a growth mindset, seeing setbacks as opportunities for improvement rather than as failures.

Taking risks and stepping into the unknown fosters resilience and self-assurance. With each attempt, children and adults learn to manage both the highs of success and the lows of setbacks, building an emotional resilience that equips them to handle life's challenges with a positive outlook. Over time, this repeated exposure to risk—and the ability to learn from it—leads to greater self-confidence. Those who embrace risk-taking come to understand that setbacks aren't permanent and can actually lead to better outcomes in the long run. It also solidifies a deep understanding that worthwhile achievements often require multiple attempts, and that persistence is as crucial as talent or knowledge.

Ultimately, by encouraging yourself and children to take calculated risks, you create a foundation for lifelong learning. Risk-taking becomes not just a tool for success but a way to fully engage with life, where each new experience—whether it's in the kitchen, in business, in travel, or in any other realm—is seen as a valuable chapter in personal growth. This mindset empowers individuals to pursue their goals, to be unafraid of failure, and to continuously refine their skills, knowing that each risk taken is another step forward on the path to becoming a resilient and successful SPOILED Producer.

Producers 2.7:

Design Thinking

Design thinking is a powerful problem-solving approach that combines empathy, creativity, and practicality to arrive at innovative solutions. At its core, design thinking is structured around five stages: empathizing with users, defining the problem, ideating solutions, prototyping, and testing. Originally developed in fields like engineering and product design, this approach has since expanded across industries and disciplines, becoming a versatile framework that can be applied to challenges big and small.

In design thinking, the *empathizing stage* is about deeply understanding the experiences, desires, and challenges of the end-users or people involved. This might mean, for example, spending time observing how a family member uses a shared space or interviewing someone about their preferences before designing a gift for them. Empathy is essential to design thinking because it shifts the focus from creating a solution based on assumptions to creating one that truly meets the needs of those it's intended to serve. When you teach children or adults to think empathetically, they learn to see the world from multiple perspectives, developing compassion as well as insight.

Next, in the *define phase*, you clearly articulate and diagnose the problem based on the insights gained during empathizing. This helps narrow down broad or vague issues into a clear, actionable problem. For example, instead of aiming to "organize a room better," a clearer problem might be defined as, "How might we create more accessible storage for frequently used items in a small space?" By defining the problem carefully, the design thinking approach ensures that solutions are directly aligned with real needs rather than vague goals.

The *ideation* phase then allows participants to brainstorm a range of possible solutions. This is where creativity shines, as individuals think freely and divergently, considering out-of-the-box ideas. Encourage children, friends, or family members to brainstorm without judgment at this stage, focusing on quantity over quality. Techniques like mind mapping, sketching, or even playful games like "What if?" can stimulate innovative thinking. For instance, when planning a family event, ideation might mean imagining every possible activity that could appeal to everyone involved, without filtering any ideas out prematurely. This stage teaches flexibility and open-mindedness—two key traits of any successful producer.

Once ideas are generated, *prototyping* brings them into the real world in a tangible form. In design thinking, a prototype doesn't have to be perfect; it can be a rough draft, a sketch, or a simple model that demonstrates the core idea. Prototyping is about creating a version of the solution that can be experienced, tested, and improved upon. A child, for instance, might prototype a new room setup by rearranging items around and experimenting with different storage methods. Prototyping is where ideas meet reality, and it shows budding producers that even an imperfect first attempt has value—it's a step toward a refined solution.

Finally, in the *testing phase*, the prototype is put to the test to see how well it meets the needs identified in the beginning. This involves asking for feedback and observing how the solution performs in real-world use. Testing reinforces the importance of refining ideas rather than expecting perfection on the first try. When children, for instance, test their room organization prototype, they might find that some items are still hard to reach or that certain arrangements aren't as practical as they seemed. Testing teaches resilience and adaptability, as it's often necessary to return to previous stages—empathizing, defining, ideating, or prototyping—to refine the solution based on new insights.

By applying design thinking in daily life, individuals learn to solve problems in a structured, thoughtful way. For example, a family member could use this approach to design a birthday gift that's personalized and truly meaningful, considering what the recipient enjoys, brainstorming creative ideas, and testing small elements to ensure the gift resonates. Similarly, planning a family event could be transformed into an engaging design thinking project where each family member contributes ideas, builds prototypes of activities, and even tests some options beforehand to see which ideas work best.

Design thinking also fosters a producer's mindset by promoting *systematic problem-solving*, where every obstacle is approached with curiosity and an openness to iterating on ideas. This method is invaluable for a producer because it encourages continuous improvement, showing that great ideas rarely come fully formed. Instead, they evolve through cycles of learning, experimenting, and refining.

By practicing design thinking, both children and adults build a toolkit for tackling challenges with *creativity, empathy, and resilience*—skills that go beyond any specific project and apply to all aspects of life. Whether creating art, starting a small business, or even just organizing a room, design thinking empowers the SPOILED Kids to produce solutions that are both innovative and grounded in real needs, creating value in any endeavor they undertake.

Producers 2.8:

Teach the Value of Contributing to Community

SPOILED Producers often look beyond personal gains, recognizing that true value lies in creating something that benefits others. A community-centered approach to production involves engaging in projects that contribute to the well-being of others, fostering a broader sense of purpose and connection. One way to practice this is by identifying specific needs within the community and taking action to address them. For example, consider creating art or decorations for a neighborhood event, designing informational materials for a local awareness campaign, or helping to organize a community garden where neighbors can come together and enjoy fresh produce. These actions not only beautify and support the community but also build pride and togetherness among participants.

Another impactful way to put a producer's mindset into action is by volunteering one's skills for local charities or nonprofit organizations. If someone has a talent for writing, they could help craft stories or content that promote a charity's cause, drawing attention and resources to their efforts. Or, if they are skilled in areas like design, coding, or tutoring, they could offer these services to organizations that may otherwise not have access to them. This type of contribution can expand an individual's understanding of how their unique skills can serve a larger mission, helping them grow as responsible and impactful producers.

SPOILED Producers can also create content that educates or inspires others, such as starting a blog, podcast, or online channel that shares valuable insights, skills, comedic entertainment, or stories. This could include anything from creating educational content on financial literacy to sharing recipes, travel tips, or tutorials that others may find beneficial. By producing content that adds value, they not only build a platform for their own voice but also provide guidance and inspiration to a wider audience. Even simple efforts like making informative social media posts about sustainable living, mental health, or community events can have a ripple effect, inspiring others to take positive action.

Our daughters have a natural affinity for social media. From a young age, they would eagerly grab a phone, filming themselves "teaching" an imaginary audience about some fascinating topic they'd discovered. They'd dress up, stand confidently in front of the camera, and describe their outfits, explaining how these choices made them feel beautiful, powerful, and unique. Watching their enthusiasm and passion for self-expression, we encouraged them to start their own channel. This became a platform for them to share all kinds of insights, from style and self-expression to their interests and our family's diverse global experiences.

Through this channel, our daughters do more than just entertain—they inspire. They've become a positive voice in their community, encouraging their audience to think beyond the ordinary and step out of the box of complacency. They share stories of adventure, determination, and family, showing that life's possibilities are boundless when approached with curiosity and courage. They discuss how the support of family, the importance of hard work, and the thrill of exploring new places can transform lives. By modeling for others what it looks like to live fully and fearlessly, they invite their audience to join in the journey.

Their channel is a reminder to young viewers that each person has a voice worth sharing and a story worth telling. It's not just about the latest trends or destinations, but about creating a life filled with meaning, connection, and exploration. Their platform encourages their community to appreciate the richness of life, build strong relationships, and pursue their dreams with confidence. In essence, our daughters are using social media to cultivate a global community that values family, empowerment, and the beauty of stepping into one's potential. Through every video, they're inspiring others to be bold, live authentically, and embrace the world with open hearts and minds.

Embracing a community-focused producer's mindset teaches individuals—children and adults alike—that producing is about more than individual gain; it's about creating meaningful impact. By seeing firsthand how their contributions can make a difference, they learn that their talents and efforts are a force for positive change. This mindset also fosters a deep sense of purpose, as they come to understand that true success includes lifting others up and making a lasting impact. Through community-focused production, individuals grow not just as creators, but as compassionate, committed citizens who actively shape a better world.

Producers 2.9:

Build an "Idea Bank"

SPOILED Producers stay energized and inspired by actively cultivating and nurturing ideas. This habit of idea generation—whether recording thoughts in a notebook, a digital document, or even an "idea jar"—keeps creativity flowing and ensures that good concepts aren't lost or forgotten. Make this a family ritual: encourage everyone to contribute ideas, no matter how big or small, wild or practical. This could include business concepts, art projects, community service ideas, or simple improvements to daily life. By involving the whole family, you create a collective idea pool that grows richer as each member adds their unique perspective and thoughts.

Set regular times to revisit this collection of ideas. Use these sessions to discuss each one's potential, brainstorm additional details, and evaluate its feasibility. Decide together which ideas to develop further, setting goals or timelines to bring them to life. These discussions don't just promote creativity—they also strengthen family bonds, as each person learns to value and build on one another's insights.

Reflecting on ideas and planning action steps builds a mindset that moves seamlessly from thought to execution. It teaches children the value of dreaming big while instilling the discipline of follow-through. Plus, by fostering a safe space for innovation, you normalize trial and error, showing that some ideas might not work out and that's okay. What matters is the willingness to explore, experiment, execute, and learn. This process inspires a lifelong habit of curiosity, resilience, and action-oriented thinking, making every family member feel like a capable, empowered producer.

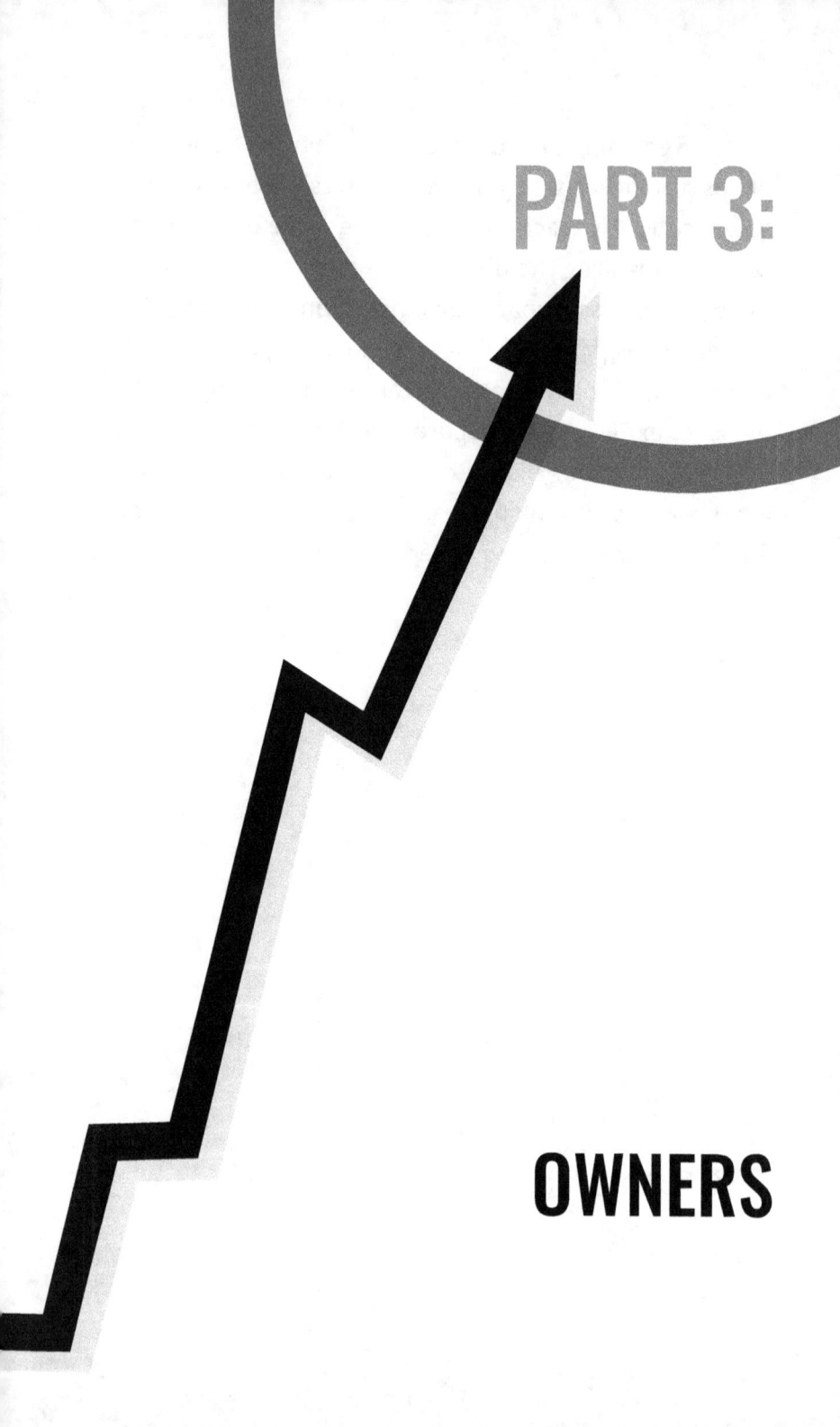
PART 3:

OWNERS

Ownership is more than possessing things; it's the responsibility that comes with having control over something. At its core, ownership requires both stewardship and accountability, ensuring that what we have—whether tangible or intangible—is used wisely, protected, and nurtured for growth. Too often ownership is equated with possessions or things—what we have, hold, or acquire. It is all the stuff that we get to play with, drive, touch, turn on or off. From a child's first toy to an adult's first home, the concept of owning something tangible is deeply ingrained in how we perceive success. However, true ownership goes beyond material possessions; it's about responsibility, accountability, and stewardship of all that we have. Ownership is not just about acquiring things; it is about taking pride in what you have, respecting its value, and being intentional about its care.

To truly own something is to care for it, improve it, and understand its value—not just in monetary terms, but in the meaning and purpose it brings to our lives. Ownership comes alive when we connect with what we possess and take responsibility for its upkeep and longevity.

We'll never forget the pride and joy we felt when we bought our first car as a married couple. It wasn't just any car; it was a milestone, a representation of our shared success and commitment. Before then, we were driving older vehicles, each holding on by a thread, and the idea of upgrading felt both necessary and symbolic. But this car wasn't just a mode of transportation—it was going to be the vehicle that carried our growing family safely through life's journeys. We imagined our baby's car seat snugly strapped in the back, keeping her safe and secure as we ventured into parenthood.

What made this purchase even more special was how intentional we were about it. Early in our marriage, we made a promise to grow our family without being weighed down by excessive debt. This meant making sacrifices and creating a detailed plan to save enough money to buy a car outright. The process wasn't easy; it required discipline, patience, and teamwork. But the day we walked into the dealership, the payoff was undeniable.

Salespeople enthusiastically tried to upsell us, offering shinier, newer models with all the bells and whistles—if only we'd take out a loan. They reminded us we were qualified for financing, but we stood firm. With quiet smiles and unwavering confidence, we politely declined and stayed within the parameters we'd set. Low miles, a non-smoking previous owner, safety features for the car seat, and a clean bill of health from our trusted mechanic—those were our non-negotiables. When we found the perfect vehicle, we negotiated the price, and then came the moment we had worked so hard for: we laid the full amount in cash on the table.

The pride we felt in that moment wasn't just about buying the car; it was about sticking to a plan, honoring our values, and achieving a shared goal. It was a tangible reminder of what we could accomplish together. But ownership didn't stop there. Owning the car meant taking care of it to to ensure its value would last. We committed to regular oil changes, tire rotations, and cleanings—especially during harsh winters to prevent rust. Each act of care reinforced not just the physical condition of the car but also the sense of pride and responsibility we felt toward it.

This experience taught us that ownership is more than acquisition. It's about stewardship—taking what you have and maximizing its worth by nurturing and maintaining it. Whether it's a car, a home, or a relationship, true ownership demands intention, care, and an ongoing commitment to improvement.

Ownership expands beyond possessions to include intangible things like ideas, goals, and commitments. We teach our children that they are the sole owners of their bodies, minds, and spirits. No external force or entity has control over those possessions and they need to take care of them as they would any particular *thing* that they own. For example, we instill that our children need to take complete ownership of their education. This doesn't just mean showing up to class; it means actively participating, asking questions, showing up prepared, completing assignments on time, seeking help when needed, and taking responsibility for their learning journey. They are expected to explore beyond the classroom and make real world connections that most likely won't show up on any assessment at school, but perhaps will be quite useful in their global travels or even differentiate them among their peers in some meaningful way. We tell them often, "the school is a place to facilitate education, but the school does not *own* your education you do!" Our children are taught that they are not to be passengers on the route to their future, rather, they own their future by investing in it and steering it themselves today.

Similarly, an entrepreneur owns their vision. They pour effort into every detail of their business, from the initial idea to its execution, understanding that their success hinges on their willingness to take responsibility for outcomes—good or bad. In order to have a Savers Mindset, one must own the goals that the savings represent, and do all that they can to commit to it to cause it to manifest. An investor owns their choices and does not shift the responsibility or blame others for what they have chosen to invest in. They take ownership even when the outcome isn't what was expected and move on to learn from the experience. A leader who embraces accountability for their team's success embodies ownership by investing in the growth of others. When the team succeeds that leader takes ownership and pride that they helped their team win. However, when the team falls short a leader with an ownership mindset will take that as an opportunity to improve themselves rather than blame the team for the failure. Mistakes and challenges are inevitable, but owning them is what sets leaders apart. When someone admits an error and takes steps to rectify it, they demonstrate integrity and maturity. This level of ownership builds trust, strengthens relationships, and paves the way for personal and professional growth.

SPOILED Ownership as both a mindset and a practice is what we will explore at depth throughout this section. By understanding the connection between what we possess and the responsibility that comes with it, we can cultivate a sense of pride and purpose. Whether owning material goods, personal goals, or collective outcomes, ownership is the foundation for building confidence, creating value, and leading a life of impact. It is often about the small acts that are the building blocks of understanding larger ownership responsibilities later in life.

By cultivating a mindset of ownership, we empower ourselves and others to take control of our lives and contribute meaningfully to the world. Having this mindset helps you and your children be more invested in the outcome, understanding that their personal contribution affects the whole team's success. Their actions show that ownership is not about titles or roles but about attitude and commitment. This approach will show up in your children's lives, among other things, as a more willingness to confidently take initiative, seeing a problem and working to solve it, rather than waiting for instructions, or permission. This exemplifies ownership, but also an understanding of how to utilize and recognize their power.

Ownership is not just something we hold; it is something we embody. It is the foundational principle of saving, producing, investing, leadership, entrepreneurship, the cornerstone of success, and a critical element of the *SPOILED Kids Mindset* overall. In this section, we will explore how to foster a culture of ownership and help you learn how to instill this essential value for your entire family.

Owners 3.1:

Ownership Mindset

As parents, we often feel an immense responsibility to manage nearly every aspect of our children's lives. It seems natural to assume that we must make all the critical decisions for them—after all, our own beliefs, rituals, attitudes, values, and experiences have shaped our sense of what it takes to succeed. This mindset, while well-intentioned, can unintentionally limit our children's growth and autonomy. Over time, we began to realize that much of our parenting approach was rooted in the programming we had inherited, shaped by cultural norms, societal expectations, and even our own childhood experiences.

This awakening wasn't easy. It required us to take a hard look at the paradigms that guided our decisions. Were we truly empowering our children, or were we unintentionally creating a dependency on our guidance? Were we equipping them with the tools to think critically, take ownership, and make confident decisions for themselves, or were we stifling their ability to develop these skills by deciding everything for them?

To embrace a *SPOILED* Mindset, we had to redefine our role as parents. Instead of being the sole decision-makers, or the ultimate decision makers in every situation, we instead chose to become guides and facilitators, empowering our children to embrace the concepts of being:

- **Savers** who understood the value of money and how to manage it wisely, even from a young age.
- **Producers** who contributed to the household or community through creativity, effort, and collaboration.
- **Owners** of their actions, choices, and responsibilities, learning accountability through everyday tasks.
- **Investors** of their time, energy, and resources, understanding that every decision has potential consequences and rewards.
- **Leaders** who could confidently make decisions, influence others positively, and stand firm in their values.
- **Entrepreneurs** who learned to recognize opportunities, solve problems, and take initiative.
- **Disciplined individuals** who have the habits and mindset needed to achieve their goals.

To make this shift, we had to adjust not only our parenting practices but also our mindset about what it truly means to guide and empower our children.

We stopped seeing ourselves as the protectors of every detail and began inviting our children to actively participate in decisions that directly affected their lives. This was not an easy transition—it required us to rethink how we used our power as parents.

In our society, power is often equated with control, especially when people are faced with challenges or obstacles. As parents, it's easy to lean on the "because I said so" approach, using authority to assert hierarchy and enforce cultural or societal norms. This tactic serves its purpose, particularly in moments of urgency or when safety and non-negotiable rules are at stake. For example, if a child decides they want to skip school to play video games, most parents would instinctively "pull rank" to ensure they fulfill their responsibility to attend school. The conversation might look something like this: "Turn off the game, get dressed, grab your bookbag, and get in the car—because you *are* going to school!" In this situation, the parent's authority and decisiveness are crucial, as children often lack the maturity and foresight to make choices that align with their long-term well-being.

However, relying solely on this top-down approach can create unintended consequences. Children are perceptive, and they quickly pick up on the tension between what we preach and what we practice. While we might tell them we want them to take responsibility, think critically, and make good decisions, our actions often leave little room for them to develop these skills. By overpowering their choices at every turn, we risk undermining their ability to process situations, weigh options, and take ownership of the outcomes.

Take the example of a child wanting to stay home from school. On the surface, it might seem like simple rebellion or laziness, but their reason often stems from a desire to avoid discomfort. Maybe they dread a difficult test, a challenging peer relationship, or the monotony of the classroom. Instead of facing these challenges, they opt for the instant gratification of staying home, playing video games, and enjoying the comfort of their own space. Can we blame them? Don't we, as adults, often feel the same way? How many mornings have we longed to stay in bed, avoiding office politics, gridlocked traffic, or the demands of our daily grind?

The difference is that adults often have the freedom to make those decisions—and the ability to weigh the consequences. We might take a day off work to recharge, knowing it will affect our productivity, but we understand the trade-off and accept responsibility for it. Children, however, don't yet have the capacity to fully evaluate these dynamics. They need guidance not just in what decisions to make but in *how* to make them.

This realization led to significant growth in our household. We began to see that teaching ownership requires more than simply dictating rules and expecting compliance. It involves creating opportunities for our children to process all sides of an argument, evaluate their choices, and understand the consequences of their actions. Instead of simply forcing compliance, we started asking more questions: "Why do you want to stay home today? What's making school feel difficult? How can we work together to address these challenges while still meeting your responsibilities?"

Through this approach, we weren't just telling our children what to do; we were equipping them with the tools to navigate their emotions, consider the bigger picture, and make informed decisions. It's not about relinquishing authority—it's about using our power differently. By guiding instead of dictating, we are helping our children develop the confidence and skills they need to take ownership of their choices and learn from their experiences. What we must realize as parents is that we must relinquish our control and sense that we own our children's decisions, when in essence, even if they comply with our every whim and wish, it's still a decision made solely by them.

This shift wasn't about letting go of our role as parents; it was about evolving it. We realized that true leadership in parenting isn't about control—it's about empowerment. When we teach our children how to think critically, act responsibly, and embrace the consequences of their decisions, we set them on a path to becoming disciplined, capable, and self-reliant individuals. This is the essence of living a *SPOILED* life—one where power is shared wisely, and responsibility is embraced fully.

Owners 3.2:

Ownership Takes CASH

Creating a *SPOILED* household requires a conscious effort to step back and use every moment as an opportunity to teach and model valuable life skills. In our home, we focus on helping our children adopt an *asset-minded* approach to life, meaning they learn to see every person, experience, and encounter as an opportunity to both *extract* and *contribute* value. The goal is to train them to see the world not just as a place to consume but as one where they can invest, grow, and thrive.

To make this concept tangible, we use the metaphor of a bank. A bank is a place where valuable assets are stored and safeguarded. When we deposit money into a bank, we know it's secure and available when we need it. The more we deposit, the more we can withdraw. In the same way, each of us is a kind of bank—a vessel capable of holding and cultivating tremendous value.

But what kind of deposits do we make into this internal bank? We teach our children that they must regularly and intentionally deposit things like self-love, positivity, discipline, creativity, knowledge, work ethic, joy, resilience, and a sense of responsibility. When they do, they build a surplus of internal wealth—one that allows them to face life's challenges without seeking external scapegoats or excuses. This "bank balance" grows over time, compounding interest with each deposit, making them stronger, wiser, and more capable.

To keep this metaphor alive, we encourage our children to "deposit CASH" into their internal bank daily. **CASH** stands for Commitment, Attitude, Sacrifice, and Hard Work.

- **Commitment**: Commitment is the unwavering dedication to one's goals and values, regardless of the obstacles or difficulties encountered along the way. It's about staying focused on the bigger picture, even when distractions, setbacks, or doubts arise. True commitment requires resilience and the ability to persevere when the excitement of starting something new fades. It's the daily decision to align actions with values, ensuring that every step, no matter how small, moves closer to the desired outcome. For children, this might mean sticking with a challenging math problem, practicing for a recital, or consistently showing up for a team, even when they'd rather quit.

- **Attitude**: Attitude is the lens through which we view the world and our circumstances. A positive, resilient outlook transforms challenges into opportunities for growth and learning. It's not about denying difficulties but rather choosing to approach them with confidence and curiosity. A strong attitude involves self-talk that encourages instead of criticizes, and the belief that every failure is a stepping stone toward success. For children, maintaining the right attitude might mean bouncing back after a tough game, trying again after a poor test score, or finding joy in small victories along the way.

- **Sacrifice**: Sacrifice is the ability to delay immediate gratification in favor of long-term rewards. It's about understanding that great achievements often come at the cost of temporary comfort or pleasure. Sacrifice teaches children to prioritize their goals over distractions, whether it's spending extra time studying instead of playing video games or saving allowance for a meaningful purchase rather than spending it impulsively. It's a powerful lesson that the most meaningful rewards require effort and the willingness to forgo what's easy for what's worthwhile.

- **Hard Work**: Hard work is the engine that drives success. It's the consistent application of effort and focus to accomplish meaningful tasks and achieve goals. Hard work means showing up, even on days when motivation is low, and pushing through discomfort or fatigue to see things through to completion. It's about doing more than the minimum—putting in the hours to improve a skill, master a subject, or make a difference. For children, hard work can manifest in practicing an instrument until they perfect a song, training rigorously for a sport, or taking the initiative to help out at home without being asked. Hard work is the bridge between aspirations and achievement, and it builds character, discipline, and confidence.

A *SPOILED Ownership Mindset* is one that fully appreciates the amount of "*CASH*" required to take responsibility for one's life, experiences, and choices. It's a mindset that helps our children recognize the value of ownership—not just over possessions but over their decisions, emotions, and future. When children internalize this approach, they grow into individuals who are empowered, resourceful, and resilient.

This mindset isn't just about success; it's about reducing unnecessary suffering. "Wait a minute," you might say, "isn't suffering an unavoidable part of the human experience? Didn't Friedrich Nietzsche famously say, *'To live is to suffer'*?" Yes, but we remind our children that the second part of Nietzsche's quote reads, *'To survive is to find meaning in that suffering.'*

This is where mindset matters most. To us,

suffering isn't just about pain or struggle—it's about how we perceive and respond to it. When we take ownership of our challenges and view them through an asset-minded lens, we can extract meaning and value from even the hardest experiences. This requires intentional thinking, resilience, and yes, plenty of *CASH*.

By normalizing these lessons and weaving them into daily life, we create a household where ownership and responsibility become second nature. Whether it's helping our children set goals, reflect on their choices, or work through setbacks, we're equipping them with the tools to live a life rooted in abundance, meaning, and joy. And while life will always present difficulties, they'll approach those challenges not as victims of circumstance but as empowered individuals with a lot of CASH stored in their internal banks. This is how they are ready to grow, learn, and thrive.

In a *SPOILED* household, every moment is a chance to deposit value—building a legacy of personal ownership and a life free from the needless suffering that comes from avoiding responsibility. Because in the end, the more purpose behind each deposit that is made with commitment, high vibrational attitudes, sacrifices the good for the great, and is met with hard work will inevitably make your children healthier, and wealthier. This is how we are instilling an ownership mindset within our children.

This shift also required letting go of the fear

that they might fail. We learned to see failure not as an endpoint, but as a valuable teacher. By allowing our children to experience setbacks in a safe and supportive environment, we are equipping them to navigate challenges with resilience and confidence.

Adopting the *SPOILED Ownership* framework in our parenting has been transformative—not only for our children but for us as well. It has shown us the power of stepping back and allowing our children to step forward, helping them develop the skills and mindset needed to thrive. In embracing this approach, we've not only redefined what it means to be parents but we also are empowering our children to build lives rooted in responsibility, independence, and purpose. They are learning to truly take ownership over their lives.

Owners 3.3:

Shifting from Protect to Prepare

When our youngest daughter was six years old, we took a week-long vacation to a friend's summer home in Florida. The house was beautiful, meticulously maintained, and featured a stunning swimming pool under a well-designed screen enclosure called a lanai. It was also just a short distance from the beach on the Gulf of Mexico. Despite the allure of the nearby ocean, our daughters spent most of the vacation in the pool, morning, noon, and night. It was their paradise.

Our six-year-old, however, didn't yet know how to swim well. She was fearless, though, and loved the water. To keep her safe, we encouraged her to stay in the shallow end, far from the "deep" end of five feet. As parents, we understood the dangers of a small child venturing into water deeper than she could handle, so we set firm boundaries. Naturally, she protested. If you know our youngest, you know she is precocious, determined, and constantly comparing herself to her older siblings. She's not one to simply "wait her turn" or let time and experience naturally prepare her for a challenge. Her determination is her hallmark—and on this vacation, it was on full display.

After much pleading and persistence, she finally won the battle to venture into the deeper end of the pool. Reluctantly, we agreed but set conditions: her two older sisters would be in the pool with her, ready to assist if anything went wrong. With her newfound permission, she eagerly jumped into the deep end, her face beaming with excitement. At first, she swam confidently, heading for the other side of the pool. But halfway across, her energy flagged, and she began to sink. Panic overtook her, and she flailed desperately, trying to keep her head above water.

Her oldest sister sprang into action, quickly grabbing her and guiding her to safety. Once out of the pool, our youngest was visibly upset—and furious. She turned on her sister, shouting, "What took you so long? You were supposed to save me!" Her tirade lasted about a minute before we gently called her over. Hugging her to calm her down, we said, "We know you're upset, but once you feel ready, you need to jump back in that pool and swim to the other side."

She glared at us. "But Zyla didn't help me! She took too long to help me."

We knelt to meet her eye level and said firmly, "Listen, sweetheart, it wasn't your sister's responsibility to save you. You have to save you. That's why it's so important to be prepared. You can make it across, we can see now that you are capable. But when it got tough, you gave up and expected someone to do the work for you. You can accept help, but never expect help. Because if that help doesn't come, you're gonna sink. If you're going to jump into deep waters, you need to make sure you're ready to follow through."

It was a harsh lesson for a six-year-old, no doubt. But it was also a vital one. About half an hour later, we heard the splash. She had jumped back in. This time, she swam to the other side by herself. Proud parent moment!

At that moment, we weren't teaching her how to swim; we were teaching her something far more profound. We weren't telling her she was alone in life or that she couldn't depend on others. On the contrary, we wanted her to know that she is surrounded by people who love her and will support her regardless of the challenges she may face in life. But we also wanted her to understand the power of mindset—specifically, a mindset of ownership. She had chosen to jump into the deep end, and she needed to take responsibility for ensuring she was ready to succeed.

This lesson is one that echoes through life. One day, she will face challenges that require risk and courage. Well-meaning people might tell her she isn't ready or try to shield her from failure, embarrassment, or disappointment. But she will have to assess her preparedness and decide for herself whether to take the leap. She will have to own her choices and the responsibility that comes with them. It certainly was a hard way to learn a lesson, but when we now ask,

"Who's responsibility is it to save you?" All three of them shout back, "Me!"

One of the most devastating scenarios we can imagine as parents is our daughters, as adults, feeling paralyzed by helplessness in the face of a challenge. We shudder at the thought of them freezing in moments that call for creativity, resilience, and action, waiting for someone else to step in and save the day. It's not that we don't believe in the value of community or the importance of asking for help—far from it. What we fear is that they might adopt a mindset that if no one comes to their rescue, their only option is to sink.

We don't want them live within a narrative of dependence, one that says, "If the government doesn't step in, I'm out of options," or "If mom and dad don't bail me out, I'm stuck," or "My friend didn't show up, so I can't make it," or worse, "I lost my home because the program denied my request for help." These are the stories of waiting for someone else to solve their problems, stories that strip away their sense of agency and leave them powerless.

Instead, we are fiercely committed to instilling an ownership mindset. It's a mindset that shifts the focus inward, reminding them that while external help is a gift and can make the journey easier, *they* are their own primary source of rescue. We want them to embrace the truth that they are responsible for their own outcomes, no matter what obstacles stand in their way or what assistance they receive—or don't receive—from others.

This ownership mindset doesn't mean they can't lean on others when the weight is heavy. It doesn't mean they should reject help or refuse support out of pride or stubbornness. But it does mean that they understand that help is supplementary, not foundational. They are the foundation. Whether or not others step in, their responsibility remains the same: to figure out a way forward. They may need to swim, paddle, or float—but ultimately, they are in charge of staying afloat.

This lesson is not about isolation; it's about empowerment. By teaching our daughters this principle, we aim to equip them to face life's inevitable storms with courage and capability. They will know that asking for help is a strength, but waiting indefinitely for rescue is a weakness. And when they find themselves in deep waters, they will draw on the confidence and resourcefulness we've nurtured in them to take the actions necessary to reach solid ground.

As parents, letting go of control is one of the most challenging aspects of raising children. Our natural instinct is to jump in—to shield them from every potential mistake, to catch them before they fall, to rescue them the moment they seem overwhelmed. In that moment at the pool, our first impulse was to dive in ourselves, to ensure our daughter was safe and shield her from fear or failure. Of course, we had safeguards in place—her sisters were nearby, and we were close enough to intervene if things went too far over her head. But even with those measures, stepping back and allowing her to navigate her challenge was a conscious, and often uncomfortable, decision.

The urge to protect our children from missteps comes from a place of love, but it's also a delicate balancing act. Overprotection can rob them of the opportunity to grow, learn, and discover their own strength. True protection doesn't mean eliminating every risk; it means equipping them with the tools to handle the risks they will inevitably face. Our role as parents is not to remove obstacles from their path but to prepare them to navigate those obstacles with confidence and resilience.

Parenthood is a journey of constant evolution. It requires us to adjust our approach as our children grow, to trust the values we've instilled, and to believe in their ability to rise to the occasion. It demands faith—not blind faith in their perfection but faith in their capacity to learn and adapt. This balance of guidance and independence is perhaps the greatest gift we can give them: the ability to face the world with courage, knowing they are capable of standing on their own two feet.

Preparing them means more than teaching them how to succeed; it means teaching them how to fail, recover, and try again. It means showing them that ownership of their actions—both triumphs and mistakes—is the key to growth. It's about empowering them to take full responsibility for their choices and outcomes, even when those choices feel daunting. When we prepare them to take complete ownership of their lives, they, in turn, prepare themselves for the challenges they will inevitably confront.

So while the instinct to protect is powerful, the real preparation lies in allowing them to face life's deep waters. We prepare them not by preventing every struggle but by teaching them how to swim, even when the current feels strong. And in doing so, we set them on a path not just to survive but to thrive, equipped with the strength, confidence, self-reliance, and self-advocacy to navigate whatever comes their way.

Owners 3.4:

Debt Free Thinking

When we purchased our first home just six months after our wedding, we were a bit clueless—or perhaps naive—about the enormous undertaking this endeavor would be. The allure of historically low interest rates, the $8,000 first-time homebuyer tax credit, and the prospect of finally owning something entirely ours made it seem like the perfect decision. At the closing table, our real estate agent joked, "Now the bank owns you." Everyone laughed, but we exchanged nervous glances, unsure of what this really meant.

By the time the mountain of paperwork—disclosures, the deed, financial agreements—was sorted through, explained, and signed, the weight of those words hit us. It wasn't a laughing matter after all. The reality set in: the bank truly did own us, and the house we thought we'd just purchased wasn't fully ours. What we'd been taught our entire lives about ownership—the pride, the independence, the freedom—felt hollow in that moment. Of course we were proud of ourselves for crossing this milestone of home ownership, what we were told is the path to long term wealth, but instead of being or feeling like owners, we were and felt more like debtors with a 30-year contract, tethered to 360 payments before we could truly call the house ours.

What we had envisioned as a milestone—a cornerstone of the American Dream—felt more like a weight. The home, our sanctuary, our place of rest and relaxation, our future space to raise children, didn't truly belong to us. It belonged to the bank. We had simply secured the privilege of living there in exchange for years of payments, interest, and the anxiety that comes with carrying such a significant debt.

The realization unsettled us. We didn't like the feeling of being tied so tightly to the bank, and it planted a seed of determination within us. We began dreaming of ways to change this narrative permanently—to truly own, not just occupy. It was the beginning of a shift in our thinking, a drive to redefine what ownership meant for our family and our future. We had to rid ourselves of this debt, and all debt for that matter, and develop a mindset of owning, not just borrowing.

When it comes to ownership, few things are as empowering as embracing a mindset of debt-free thinking. Ownership begins not with the things you possess, but with the freedom to make choices unburdened by financial strain. Debt-free thinking isn't just a strategy for us; we've been able to make it into a lifestyle, a discipline, and a declaration that we refuse to trade your future for fleeting moments of satisfaction today.

Debt is often presented as a necessary tool—a means to an end. Society tells us we need loans to buy homes, credit cards to build financial credibility, and financing to afford cars, education, and even vacations. While some debt can be strategic, many of us fall into a pattern where debt becomes a trap rather than a tool. We overextend ourselves for things that depreciate in value, and before we know it, our income is spoken for before it even reaches our hands.

Debt robs you of options. At least it was robbing us of our desire and opportunity to travel internationally at three times yearly. It was limiting our ability to invest in business ventures. It was dictating how we spent our money and, in many cases, our time. When you're working primarily to pay off obligations, your ability to invest in ownership—of assets, opportunities, and even your own growth—becomes severely limited. To think like a SPOILED Owner, we must rethink our relationship with debt and embrace a mindset that prioritizes freedom and intentionality.

Debt-free thinking isn't just about avoiding financial obligations; it's about creating space for opportunity. When we finally unburdened ourselves from payments, we were able to:

- **Invest in Assets:** We had the ability to put our money toward things that grew in value, such as our properties, businesses, and to further education with Masters and Doctorate degrees.

- **Take Risks:** Entrepreneurship, career changes, or even taking time off to focus on personal development becomes possible when you're not living paycheck to paycheck or the paycheck is devoured by debt payment obligations.
- **Achieve True Ownership:** We were the owners not "owned" by or beholden to lenders. This meant that we truly owned what we've worked for.

A debt-free mindset creates financial resilience. Emergencies, unexpected opportunities, or even economic downturns are less likely to derail your progress when you're not tied to excessive obligations. It begins with a shift in priorities. One of the biggest contributors to unnecessary debt is failing to differentiate between what we want and what we truly need. A new car may be a want, but reliable transportation is the need. A sprawling home might be a dream, but a modest, comfortable living space is sufficient. Debt-free thinking demands clarity about these distinctions and the discipline to act accordingly.

In a world that celebrates instant gratification, debt-free thinking requires patience. You may want that designer bag, the latest tech gadget, or a luxury vacation, but the ability to wait and save for it—or decide you don't need it at all—is a hallmark of financial maturity.

Each dollar you spend is a choice and an opportunity. When you adopt a debt-free mindset, you become intentional about how you allocate your money. This means budgeting, tracking expenses, and consistently asking yourself, "Is this purchase aligned with my values and goals?" It is far easier and rewarding to know that you can pursue your values and financial goals without the weight of unnecessary debt.

The gift that you give to your children in the form of a mindset of financial independence is one of the greatest things that you can provide for them. Help them understand the power of saving, the cost of debt, and the value of ownership early. Include them in conversations about budgeting, encourage them to save for their own purchases, and model the discipline of living within your means.

By fostering debt-free thinking, you empower your children to become SPOILED Owners who understand that freedom and ownership go hand in hand. And as SPOILED Owners, we aim to redefine wealth, not just as an accumulation of assets, but as a state of mind and being. By embracing debt-free thinking, we take a crucial step toward true ownership—of our finances, our choices, and ultimately, our lives. And owning will always be greater than owing and lead to a much more enjoyable life.

Owners 3.5:

The BEST Method for Financial Freedom

For our family, the journey to becoming debt-free required a delicate blend of strategies, discipline, teamwork, and an unwavering commitment to the vision we had for our future. It was neither quick nor easy, but it was profoundly worth it. By leveraging tools like the snowball method, careful budgeting, effective spousal communication, clear priorities, diligent savings, and the practice of delayed gratification, we were able to achieve what many believe is unattainable: complete financial freedom.

When friends and family learned that we were living a debt-free lifestyle—one that allowed us to experience life fully, both domestically and internationally—they assumed we had either hit the jackpot or stumbled upon some secret fortune. They were astounded when we explained that we didn't win the lottery or receive an inheritance. In disbelief, they would ask, "How is it possible to own your home outright, drive cars without loans, carry no credit card balances, and owe nothing to anyone?" The truth is, it *is* possible. But while it's easier than many might imagine, it's also harder than we make it seem in this book.

Even as we share our methods and strategies, we want you to understand that your journey to financial freedom will be unique. You might replicate everything we did or implement just one key strategy to fit your circumstances. What matters most is finding what works for *you* and *your family*. The beauty of the debt-free lifestyle is that it's not one-size-fits-all; it's about tailoring principles to your life and committing to them.

When we began our debt-free journey, we both had steady bi-weekly paychecks directly deposited into our joint accounts. One of us carried the health insurance through our employer to maximize the take-home pay of the other. In addition to our regular salaries, we occasionally earned irregular income through speaking engagements, book sales from other publications, and consulting work. To supplement our income, one of us would take on a part-time or seasonal job. However, we were careful not to overextend ourselves or sacrifice family time and mental well-being in the process.

While having a dual-income household certainly helped us accelerate progress toward our financial goals, it wasn't the sole key to our success. What truly made the difference was our intentionality. We treated every dollar we earned as an opportunity to move closer to our goals. Whether you have one income, multiple streams, or even a modest fixed income, the principles we outline can certainly can work for you as well.

The most critical element of becoming debt-free isn't how much money you make—it's the mindset you bring to managing it. Whether you earn a six-figure salary or are working with a limited monthly budget, the key is developing a clear distinction between *wants* and *needs*. This clarity allows you to channel your resources intentionally and align your spending with your priorities.

A positive mindset is your most powerful tool. It's not just about crunching numbers or making sacrifices; it's about believing in your ability to create the life you desire. Your decision to read this book is already a testament to your commitment to personal growth and financial freedom. You've taken the first step toward building a better life for yourself and a lasting legacy for your children.

For us, this mindset shift began with education. We read every book on financial literacy we could find, listened to podcasts, devoured audiobooks, and watched countless hours of online content. We followed individuals we admired and learned from their practical insights and experiences. This process of relentless self-education became the foundation for the strategies and methods we share in this book. We didn't "invent" these strategies, rather discovered them and altered them accordingly to fit our way of thinking and lifestyle. We have listed some of our favorite content, budgeting worksheets, and other materials we've found along the way on the SPOILED Family Portal of our website www.MYSPOILEDKids.com.

    The process of becoming debt-free is deeply personal. What works for us may not work exactly the same way for you, and that's okay. The principles remain universal: live below your means, prioritize your goals, and take intentional steps toward your vision. By deciding to embark on this journey, you've already begun to rewrite your financial story. The tools and strategies in this book are designed to empower you to create a life of freedom, opportunity, and abundance. Remember, becoming debt-free isn't just about numbers on a spreadsheet—it's about transforming your mindset, your habits, and your legacy.

    We're proof that it's possible. And if we can do it, so can you. So what did we do exactly? What was it that we did to become debt-free and remain that way? We use what we call the **BEST Method for Financial Freedom**. BEST stands for *Budgeting, Eliminating Debt Landslide, Sacrifice,* and *Time*. We used the BEST Method to become debt free and still use it to remain that way.

Owners 3.6:

Budgeting

Very early in our marriage, when we were first beginning to combine our lives—bringing together two distinct sets of past experiences, habits, and philosophies about money—we realized that creating a unified financial approach would require more than just merging bank accounts. It demanded a complete rethinking of how we managed our resources and aligned our financial behavior with the family goals we were building together.

At the heart of this process was learning how to effectively create and utilize a budget. Early on, we encountered a saying that profoundly impacted us: *"Don't tell me what you value; show me your budget, and I'll tell you what you value."* Those words stuck with us because they were undeniably true. A budget isn't just numbers on a page—it's a reflection of your priorities, values, and vision for your life.

We quickly realized that before we could create a budget, we needed to define our values. What did we hold in high esteem? How did we envision living our lives? And most importantly, who mattered most to us? Answering these questions gave us clarity, purpose, and a sense of direction for our financial decisions.

Our initial attempts at budgeting were, to be honest, rudimentary and ineffective. Like many people, we started by listing all our expenses—things like the mortgage payment, credit card bills, utilities, car payments, insurance, groceries, phone bills, childcare, entertainment, and miscellaneous costs. Once we had everything listed, we added up the total and subtracted it from our combined monthly income.

If we ended up with a positive number, we treated it as "leftover" money to spend however we wanted that month. If the number was negative—and it occasionally was—we scrambled to figure out how to make ends meet. Sometimes we skipped paying one bill, scaled back on groceries, or cut down on entertainment just to ensure we had enough to cover our immediate obligations.

While this approach gave us a snapshot of our finances, it wasn't helping us achieve the long-term goals we desired. We needed a method that gave every dollar a purpose, eliminated waste, and ensured we were making intentional progress toward financial freedom. That's when we discovered the concept of the **Zero-Based Budget**.

A Zero-Based Budget fundamentally changed how we approached our finances. With this method, every dollar of income is assigned a specific purpose—whether it's for bills, savings, debt repayment, or discretionary spending—so the total income minus expenses equals zero. This doesn't mean you spend every dollar; it means every dollar is allocated. By design, there's no leftover money to fritter away or gaps that leave you scrambling.

This approach gave us complete control over our finances and helped us eliminate wasteful spending. It required discipline and meticulous planning, but the benefits were transformative. By using a Zero-Based Budget, we could plan our spending with precision, ensure no money went unaccounted for, and align our finances with our goals, especially debt elimination.

Since our primary goal was to eliminate debt, we decided to create two monthly budgets:

1. **The Household Budget**: This included variable expenses like groceries, entertainment, childcare, utilities, car maintenance, emergency funds, clothing, grooming, and other non-fixed costs. We totaled these expenses and organized them by due date to match them with our bi-weekly income.

2. **Debt Elimination, Fixed Expenses and Growth Budget**: This included items like mortgage payments, car loans, credit cards, and minimum debt payments.

To simplify things further, we dedicated the smaller of our two incomes exclusively to cover the household budget. This strategy ensured that our basic living expenses were always taken care of while allowing us to focus the larger income on debt repayment and long term growth.

- **Plan Ahead**: Take the time to review all upcoming expenses for the month, including irregular costs like birthdays, holidays, or seasonal needs.

- **Adjust Regularly**: No two months are exactly alike. Revisit your budget frequently to make adjustments for unexpected changes.

- **Stay Disciplined**: It's easy to veer off course, but remember that every dollar has a purpose. Stick to the plan and be Disciplined, you can be SPOILED without it.

Budgeting isn't just about numbers—it's about aligning your money with your values, empowering your family, and working toward a life of financial freedom. A Zero-Based Budget gave us the structure we needed to achieve our goals, and we're confident it can do the same for you. By creating a plan, sticking to it, and adapting as needed, you'll be well on your way to building a debt-free, purpose-driven future.

Bi-Weekly Income				
Bank	Routing #/ Account #	Purpose	Path	After Tax Amount
Name of Bank		Family Expenses	Direct Deposit	$1,848.18

Monthly Expenses					
Bills	Budgeted	Actual/Average	Date Due	Method/ Notes	Paid
Vacation Fund	532.20	929.93	n/a	Auto	
Groceries	350	n/a	n/a	Manual	
Fuel (2 Vehicles)	150	n/a	n/a	Manual	
Child Care	300	300	1st	Auto	
Streaming Service	15.99	15.99	5th	Auto	
Utility Bill #1	175	350	6th	Auto	
Gym Membership	24.99	24.99	10th	Auto	
"Pocket" Money	200	600	n/a	Manual	
Entertainment	100	200	n/a	Manual	
↑ Check #1			↓ Check #2		
Emergency Fund	397.73	929.93	n/a	Auto	
Groceries	350	n/a	n/a	Manual	
Fuel (2 Vehicles)	150	n/a	n/a	Manual	
Car Insurance	163.47	163.47	12th	Auto	
Cloud Storage	1.99	1.99	15th	Auto	
Car Maintenance	50	50	17th	Auto: "Car" Account	
Phone Bill	175	175	18th	Auto	
Utility Bill #2	175	350	23rd	Auto	
Internet	84.99	84.99	23rd	Auto	
"Pocket Money"	200	600	n/a	Auto	
Entertainment	100	200	n/a	Manual	
Totals					
		Monthly Income		$3,696.36	
		Monthly Expenses		$3,696.36	
		Balance		$0	

Figure 1

To make the process easier, we created a Zero-Based Budget worksheet template, which you can find in the "Resources" section of the **SPOILED Family Portal** at www.MySPOILEDKids.com. This template includes everything you need to get started, from categories for expenses to a step-by-step guide for assigning every dollar.

Owners 3.7:

Eliminating Debt Landslide

Before we understood the suffocating impact of debt, we were easily lured by the allure of instant gratification—using credit to acquire things we wanted but couldn't afford. Debt felt manageable in the short term, but over time it became a crippling obstacle. When we got married, not only did we bring shared dreams into our union, but also a significant amount of debt from our individual pasts. The baggage of yesterday became today's reality, and we knew that ignoring it wasn't an option. We needed a plan, and we needed it fast.

Through relentless research, late-night discussions, and plenty of trial and error, we developed a strategy we call the Eliminating Debt Landslide (EDL). While this method resembles approaches such as the debt snowball or debt avalanche, what we value most about the EDL is its aggressive, focused simplicity. The core idea is to tackle debt systematically, incrementally, and with intentionality until it is eradicated.

When we looked at the timeline for paying off our debts with minimum payments, the numbers were staggering:

- Mortgage: 30 years.
- Student Loans: 40 to 50 years.
- Credit Cards: Over 28 years, but possibly forever.

Those timelines weren't just unacceptable—they were barriers to the life we envisioned for ourselves and our children. Debt was robbing us of our freedom. It restricted our ability to travel the world with our kids, invest in business ventures, and decide whether to stay employed or take time off to pursue our passions. We realized that the longer we stayed tethered to debt, the further away we were from living the life we dreamed of.

With a SPOILED Ownership Mindset, we made a decision: we refused to be enslaved by debt. Instead, we chose freedom—a freedom that allowed us to live on our own terms, take risks, and build a legacy of financial independence for our family.

Step 1: Take Inventory of Your Debt

The first step to eliminating debt is simple but critical: take a hard, honest look at what you owe. Create a complete list of all your debts, including:

- Creditor names.
- Outstanding balances.
- Minimum monthly payments.
- Interest rates.

Seeing the total amount of debt might feel overwhelming, but this clarity is the first step toward taking control. Once we had this list, we designed a specific chart to organize our Eliminating Debt Landslide Plan. One thing that was also empowering for us is that we treated our future dreams as one of our creditors. This means that we listed *Investment Fund* as a line item treating it as a "debt" prepayment for our future endeavors. Treating our future investment and business goals as a "bill" helped shape our mindset around its specific purpose and helped us in the end continue to grow.

Step 2: Separate Household Expenses and Debt Payments

To maximize efficiency, we used the smaller of our two incomes to manage household expenses. This included groceries, utilities, childcare, and other day-to-day costs. The larger salary was then allocated solely to debt repayment, deposited into a separate account to avoid mixing funds.

For example:
- Monthly Income (Higher Salary): $4,000
- Total Monthly Debt Payments: $3,600
- Remaining Balance for EDL: $400

This leftover balance became our Landslide fund—the extra money we used to aggressively pay off debts beyond the minimums.

Step 3: Prioritize and Pay Strategically

We structured the EDL using a lowest balance to highest balance approach:
1. List debts by balance size, starting with the smallest.
2. Pay the minimum amount due on all debts.
3. Apply the remaining Landslide funds ($400 in this example) to the smallest debt.

Here's how it worked:
- If the smallest debt required a $200 minimum payment, we added the $400 Landslide fund to pay $600 each month. This accelerated repayment.

- Once that debt was fully paid, we rolled its payment ($600) into the next smallest debt. If the next debt's minimum payment was $225, we added the previous payment ($600) for a total of $825 per month.

- Once that is paid in full, we rolled the previous Landslide payment into the next smallest balance. If that next debt's minimum payment was $345, we added the previous Landslide payment ($825) for a new payment toward that debt of $1,170 per month.

We repeated this process for every debt, each time increasing the payment amount as debts were eliminated. By the time we reached the largest debt, we were applying the full combined debt payments and Landslide fund, which amounted to the full monthly salary, wiping out our debt far faster than we ever thought possible.

Step 4: Close Paid Accounts and Stay Focused

When we paid off a debt, we immediately closed the account. This helped us avoid the temptation to reopen lines of credit and fall back into old habits. Closing accounts also gave us a psychological boost, serving as a tangible reminder of our progress. We want to note here we kept some accounts, such as low-interest credit cards, open but cut up the physical cards. In doing so, we were strategic about protecting and growing our credit score (i.e. some employers look at credit score and debt as a metric for gaining employment). The length of time an account has been open is also an important factor in maintaining a healthy credit score

Staying disciplined was key. We automated all payments to ensure consistency, avoided accumulating new debt, and regularly reviewed our progress to stay motivated. The result was that utilizing our Eliminating Debt Landslide, we were able to eliminate over $250,000 in debt in the course of five years. What would have taken decades—and cost hundreds of thousands of dollars in additional interest—was gone in a fraction of the time. The feeling of freedom was indescribable.

Without the burden of debt, we were able to:

Invest an entire salary into savings, retirement, and wealth-building ventures.

- Take more risks with our business ideas.
- Travel to exotic destinations and create priceless memories with our children.
- Live life on our own terms, without the constant stress of financial obligations.

Our journey taught us that debt elimination isn't about how much money you make—it's about your mindset, your plan, and your execution. Sure, making more money can accelerate the process, but the key is discipline and intentionality. Even if your income is modest, a clear strategy like the EDL can dramatically shorten the time it takes to achieve financial freedom.

If we could eliminate $250,000 in debt on two modest incomes, imagine what you could achieve. The power lies not in your starting point but in your willingness to commit, sacrifice, and stay the course. Debt freedom isn't just a goal—it's a gateway to the life you've always dreamed of. Let the Eliminating Debt Landslide help you break free and reclaim your financial future. The chart on the next page is an example of the EDL in action.

Monthly Income				
Bank	Routing #/ Account #	Purpose	Path	After Tax Amount
Name of Bank		Debt Elimination and Growth	Direct Deposit	$4,526.74

Escalation Cycle				
Creditor	Total Payoff	Minimum Payment	Payment + Escalation	Payoff Period
Loan #1	5,425	225	795.74	7 months
Store Credit Card	6,050	275	1,070.74	11 months
Credit Card #1	10,250	510	1,580.74	14 months
Credit Card #2	12,400	645	2,225.74	16 months
Credit Card #3	15,700	720	2,945.74	18 months
Student Loan #1	28,750	260	3,205.74	25 months
Student Loan #2	62,000	380	3,585.74	39 months
Mortgage	115,000	841	4,426.74	59 months
Investment Fund	30,000	100	4,526.74	

Growth Plan				
Investment Fund	$30,000	100	4,526.74	64 months

OWNERS 3.8:

Sacrifice

Building something substantial for yourself, your children, and future generations is a noble goal, but it does not come without significant sacrifice. Sacrifice is the cornerstone of creating a legacy of wealth, values, and opportunities that can outlive you. If your aim is to raise children who are *Savers, Producers, Owners, Investors, Leaders, Entrepreneurs, and Disciplined* (SPOILED), you must first commit to embodying and modeling these principles in your daily life.

It's unrealistic to expect your children to delay gratification if they don't see you doing the same. If you're consistently spending money on things that bring fleeting pleasure rather than prioritizing savings and investments, they will learn to follow your example, not your words. Similarly, you cannot preach the importance of living a debt-free lifestyle while being burdened by overwhelming debt that limits not only your freedom but also theirs. Debt has a way of enslaving time and energy that could otherwise be used to create meaningful experiences, deepen relationships, or pursue dreams. To raise children who embody the SPOILED values, you must first become a SPOILED parent—one who is willing to make hard choices, prioritize long-term goals over short-term pleasures, and consistently model the mindset and habits you want your children to emulate.

This is no small task, especially in a society dominated by a culture of instant gratification. Social media bombards us daily with curated glimpses of people living lavishly, prioritizing material possessions over meaningful wealth-building. The temptation to compare and keep up with others is ever-present. However, the commitment to sacrifice is what will set your family apart. It's not easy to go against the grain, but the rewards are transformative. By rejecting the "right now" mindset and embracing intentionality, you open the door to financial freedom, family cohesion, and the ability to pass down something far more valuable than material goods—a legacy.

To truly teach and embody the concept of sacrifice, it's important to make it an active and visible part of your family's lifestyle. Sacrifice begins with learning how to say 'no' to short-term desires in favor of long-term goals. This means modeling restraint and showing your children how to prioritize needs over wants. For example, when faced with a decision to buy a new gadget or contribute to savings, explain why you're choosing to save. Say, "This money will grow and help us take a family vacation next year," or "It's important to save so we can buy our next car without going into debt." By making your thought process transparent, you teach your children the value of intentional decision-making.

We like to Involve our children in setting long-term family goals, whether it's saving for a home, paying off debt, or building an emergency fund. When we were younger there was definitely a line between "grown folks business" and a "child's place" and those role rarely crossed without some stark consequences. We have decided to blur this line to create an atmosphere of inclusivity, afterall, everyone in the house is affected by the decision that are being made. We show our children how to budget, save, and invest. For example, when we were eliminating our debts, we would often share and celebrate the progress updates in a way they could understand. We would say things like, "This month, we paid off another $500 of our mortgage. That means we're getting closer to owning this house outright!" This not only normalizes financial discipline but also helps children understand the power of sacrifice in achieving financial freedom. This also helps them understand the Ownership Mindset in a way that is real, tangible, and relatable.

Teach your children to find joy and contentment in non-material things. This starts with you. Celebrate family time, achievements, or simple pleasures like a homemade meal or a game night. Gratitude shifts the focus from what you don't have to appreciating what you do, creating a mindset of abundance rather than scarcity. This attitude helps children understand that sacrifice doesn't mean deprivation—it means focusing on what truly matters. When we were thinking about what a debt-free life would be like, we imagined that it would free up our most important resource: time. And normalizing spending this time building a stronger family bond by seizing opportunities to be together didn't have to wait.

But sacrifice isn't just about giving things up—it's also about giving to others. Show your children how to be generous with time, money, and resources. Volunteer as a family, donate to causes you care about, or help a neighbor in need. Acts of service teach children that sacrifice can enrich the lives of others and bring fulfillment in return.

When you model sacrifice in these ways, you're not just teaching your children about financial responsibility—you're giving them the tools to build their own legacies. They'll learn that true wealth isn't about having everything you want in the moment; it's about having the freedom to live a life aligned with your values and dreams. Raising SPOILED kids with an Ownership Mindset requires you to embody the principles of sacrifice and discipline in your own life. It's not easy, but it's worth it. The legacy of sacrifice is a legacy of strength, freedom, and opportunity that will ripple through generations.

Owners 3.9:

Time

It took our family over five years to completely eliminate debt—a feat that required unwavering discipline, relentless focus, and a carefully crafted strategic plan. This process not only freed us financially but also cultivated a patience within us that we continue to rely on as we work toward other goals for ourselves, our children, and the legacy we aim to leave behind.

Through this journey, we've come to deeply understand the importance of Time in the process of generational wealth-building. Time is the most valuable resource we have. Unlike money, it cannot be earned back, multiplied, or recovered once it's gone. Every second wasted is an opportunity lost—an opportunity to plant seeds, nurture growth, and move closer to our vision for the future.

We've also embraced a profound reality: the fruits of our efforts may not fully ripen in our lifetime. We may not live to see the full extent of the impact our work will have on our children, grandchildren, and great-grandchildren. And yet, we are content being the seed. A seed contains within it everything necessary to grow into a towering tree, offering shade, shelter, and sustenance for generations to come. Our role as the seed is to plant the essence of wealth, discipline, and abundance in the hearts and minds of our children, nurturing it with consistent effort, guidance, and love until the day we are no longer here.

Statistically, we are keenly aware that we have more years behind us than ahead of us, making our sense of Time even more urgent. We've adopted the mindset that time is not infinite, and therefore, every moment must serve a purpose. Whether it's teaching our children how to save, spending quality time as a family, or pursuing dreams that inspire us, we recognize that every second is an investment. Every day counts, which is why we live with what we call a "*patient urgency.*" Patient urgency means striking the delicate balance between moving with purpose and knowing that growth—true, meaningful growth—takes time.

We act with urgency in teaching our children by example every single day. Whether it's budgeting, saving, investing, or making sacrifices, we recognize that they are learning more from what we do than from what we say. However, we remain patient, knowing that just like any seed, growth is a gradual process. It takes time for roots to deepen and branches to stretch toward the sky. Building generational wealth and a legacy is not about rushing to achieve immediate results. It's about playing the long game. Just as a tree takes years to grow before it can bear fruit, the values, habits, and principles we instill in our children take time to fully manifest.

This patience doesn't mean passivity—it means working every day with purpose while trusting the process. It means accepting that not every effort will yield immediate results but knowing that every step forward, no matter how small, contributes to the greater vision.

The power of time lies in its ability to multiply efforts, especially when combined with discipline and consistency. Consider this: every minute spent procrastinating, indulging in unproductive habits, or chasing fleeting pleasures is time stolen from the future. Time wasted today compounds into missed opportunities tomorrow. But time isn't just about money. It's about relationships, memories, and the impact you leave on the world. Time spent teaching your children, mentoring them, and sharing your values is never wasted. Every lesson you impart becomes a building block in their foundation, equipping them to carry the torch of your legacy forward.

As parents, our ultimate goal is to plant seeds that will bear fruit long after we're gone. These seeds are the principles we live by, the habits we model, and the mindset we instill in our children. A seed will only grow into the tree it was designed to be—an apple seed will never produce an orange tree—the seeds we plant will determine the type of legacy we leave behind.

For us, this means planting the SPOILED Mindset—a mindset rooted in abundance, discipline, and growth. While we cannot control how "tall" or successful each child's tree will grow, we take comfort in knowing that the seeds we've planted will only yield trees of strength, resilience, and purpose. How far our children take these principles will be determined by their unique goals, dreams, and ambitions.

By understanding the value of time and teaching our children to do the same, we are equipping them with the most powerful resource they'll ever have. Time is the soil in which the seeds of wealth, discipline, and abundance grow. When managed wisely, it can create a harvest so abundant that it feeds not only the present generation but those to come. So let us never waste it. Let us teach our children the urgency of purpose and the patience of progress, for in doing so, we lay the foundation for a legacy that will endure the test of time.

And let us also remember this: time is precious not only because it is *finite*, but because within it live the echoes of those we have loved and lost. Every second carries traces of their presence—the sound of their laughter, the wisdom of their words, the warmth of their embrace. What once felt ordinary becomes sacred when they are no longer here. The shared meals, the long conversations, the quiet moments—these become treasures beyond measure, woven into the very fabric of who we are.

Their absence is a powerful reminder that tomorrow is never guaranteed and that every moment we share with those we love is a gift that will never return in quite the same way. By choosing to cherish the present—to look into the eyes of those beside us, to speak love while we have the chance, to forgive quickly and hold tightly—we not only honor the memory of those who came before us, we also teach our children the truest meaning of time. It is not measured in minutes or days, but in connection, compassion, and the legacy of love that endures long after the clock stops ticking.

In this way, those we've lost are never truly gone. They continue to live—in our stories, in our choices, and in the way we carry their love forward into the world. Every intentional moment becomes a living tribute to their memory, a bridge between what was and what can still be.

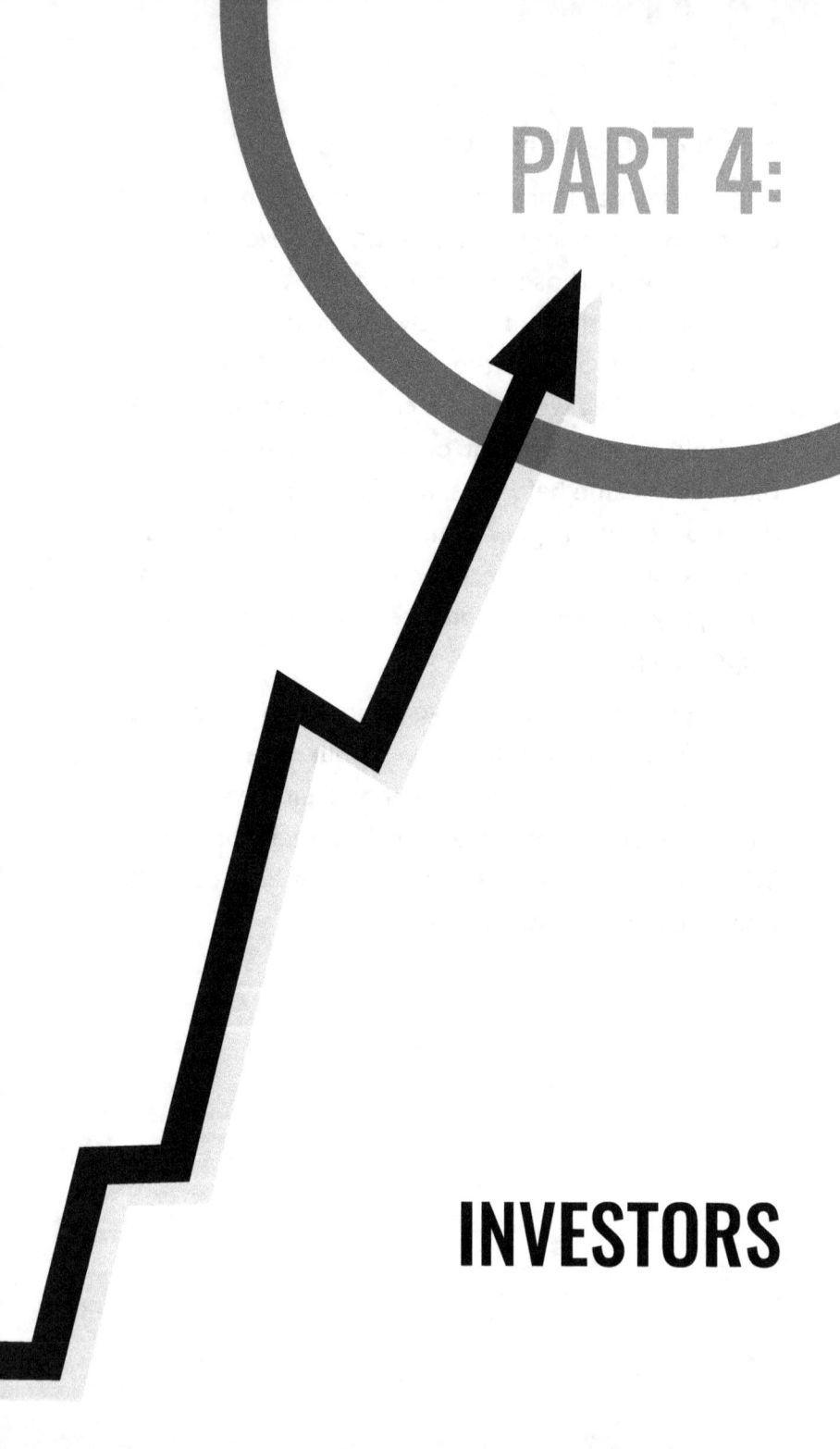

According to Investopedia, an investor is any person or entity that allocates resources—most commonly capital—with the expectation of generating financial returns. Investors utilize various strategies to achieve their financial goals, such as purchasing stocks with the hope of receiving a return on investment (ROI). At its core, investing is about putting in resources with the expectation of receiving more in return. The principle is simple: the more you invest wisely, the greater your potential to reap significant returns.

However, successful investing requires more than just putting money into something and hoping for the best. A skilled investor understands that investments are not merely transactions but calculated decisions. They involve assessing risks, analyzing data, and making informed choices while recognizing that substantial returns often require time and patience. These principles embody the essence of delayed gratification and the discipline necessary to achieve long-term financial success.

Robert Kiyosaki, the author of *Rich Dad, Poor Dad*, emphasizes this concept. He explains that the wealthiest individuals are not just earners but investors. They work hard to generate income, but they also use that income to invest in assets that, in turn, generate more money. This cycle of investment leads to passive income—the cornerstone of financial independence. Kiyosaki's *Cashflow Quadrant* simplifies this idea, categorizing income into two types: active and passive.

Active income stems from being an employee or self-employed, where money is earned through direct effort. National statistics reveal that over 63% of individuals aged 16 and older rely on employment as their primary source of income. This means their financial security depends on consistently showing up and working. On the other hand, passive income is generated through investments or businesses that require minimal ongoing effort, such as rental properties, dividends, or royalties. Approximately 20% of the working population relies on passive income as their primary source of income, leveraging the power of money to work for them.

The SPOILED Investor mindset builds on this foundation but expands it to encompass more than just financial wealth. A SPOILED Investor doesn't only think in terms of dollars and cents—they understand that investments include time, energy, relationships, and skills. The essence of being a SPOILED Investor lies in the ability to assess value, weigh risks, and focus on pursuits that deliver meaningful and lasting returns. This approach requires patience, discipline, and intentionality, ensuring that every resource is allocated strategically to align with long-term goals and core values.

Investing is about more than accumulating money—it's about making thoughtful decisions to trade something of value today for a greater reward tomorrow. For example, when you invest time into learning a new skill, the return is knowledge, which can unlock opportunities, enhance your capabilities, and broaden your potential. Similarly, financial investments are rooted in understanding and evaluating potential returns, whether through a company's growth or a portfolio's performance.

The SPOILED Investor framework emphasizes this multifaceted approach. It teaches that when you invest intentionally—whether it's time, money, or effort—you are setting the stage for exponential growth. Investments, when chosen wisely and aligned with your values, have the power to work for you, multiplying their benefits and freeing you to focus on what truly matters in life. In the SPOILED Investor journey, you become the master of your resources, empowering them to serve you rather than being enslaved by the constant grind of earning and spending. Through this framework, we aim to instill a mindset that moves beyond the transactional nature of traditional investing. Instead, it nurtures a holistic perspective where every decision—financial or otherwise—is viewed as an investment in your future self, your family, and your legacy. A SPOILED Investor understands that the greatest returns come not only from financial growth but also from personal and collective fulfillment.

INVESTORS 4.1:

The Investor Mindset

The SPOILED Investor's Mindset is about cultivating a strategic, thoughtful approach to making choices that lead to long-term growth and abundance. This mindset focuses on the ability to think ahead, evaluate risks and rewards, and understand the value of calculated sacrifice. It's a mentality that goes beyond money, instilling a way of thinking that can help young people build a fulfilling life by learning to make informed decisions, prioritize wisely, and develop resilience in the face of challenges.

At the heart of the Investor's Mindset is an understanding that any investment requires sacrifice—whether it's time, energy, money, or comfort. They must know and understand that everything has a cost. Nothing is ever free. And when the SPOILED Investor is willing to pay the costs associated with that in which they desire, they then must understand that the sacrifices that yield desired rewards are often accompanied by risks.

The Investor's Mindset teaches kids to weigh risks against potential rewards thoughtfully. It's about understanding that every choice has potential upsides and downsides, and learning to navigate these possibilities with clarity. This skill helps in decision-making not only in financial situations but also in personal life, where choosing friends, managing time, or taking on responsibilities requires careful consideration.

A child with an Investor's Mindset might decide whether to join an extracurricular activity based on how it aligns with their interests and goals. They weigh the time commitment against the potential learning and fun they'll gain, making a balanced decision. The goals that SPOILED Investors have in mind should be able to benefit them in the near and long-term future, and they must be thinking about how it aligns with other aspects of their life.

Investors are inherently goal-oriented. The Investor's Mindset trains kids to set meaningful goals and think ahead. They learn to envision what they want to achieve, whether it's financial security, educational success, or personal growth, and to map out steps toward those goals. Long-term thinking also promotes patience and commitment, showing them that most achievements take time and effort.

When our oldest daughter wanted a new phone, an upgrade from her flip phone we bought her, she communicated her desires with us. She came prepared with a plan complete with the vast reasons why an updated device was valuable for her other goals. Part of her plan was that she would use a portion of her savings to invest in starting a business doing hair for friends and family. We were excited to take her to the beauty supply wholesale warehouse so that she could buy the necessary equipment and tools she would need for her business. We then, by chance, found a barber down the street from our house that was moving and selling some of their equipment. We invested in her business by purchasing professional hair drying and barbering chairs. We repurposed the playroom to be her salon.

 Each time she would braid her sister's hair we would pay her a rate nearly equivalent to what we would pay others to do the same. She would get paid doing her mother's hair, her cousin's and her friend's hair, creating wonderful new patterns and experimenting with styles that brought smiles to her customers. She not only thoroughly enjoyed her work, but had a sense of accomplishment and ownership working her business. Her Investor's Mindset encouraged her to think creatively about how to maximize the resources available to her and enhance them to make something better. She was learning to look beyond traditional paths and discover innovative ways to solve problems, create value, and turn opportunities into tangible outcomes.

 Each week she would put money into her savings account to replace her investments and continue growing it until she reached her goal. She was diligent and focused on her plan. When the opportunity arose to spend her money going out with friends, or the temptation to buy snacks each day after school or other items, she resisted. She would say that these sacrifices were worth it to get to her goal. Delayed gratification is a core part of the Investor's Mindset. This principle taught her to resist the urge for immediate rewards in favor of greater benefits later on. It instilled self-discipline and showed her that her choices today will impact her in the future.

By consistently saving, the SPOILED Kid learns to plan for larger achievements over time rather than only enjoying the rewards of the present. Of course, we encourage our children to have a healthy social life, and a balanced approach to life, so along her journey to her goal of a new phone, we would pay for outings and fun events with her friends and extended family. Afterall, she is still a kid, a SPOILED kid, but a kid nonetheless.

No investment is without risk, and sometimes, things don't go as planned. There were weeks when her obligations as a student, athlete, a member of our traveling family, or when her "new style" failed to meet the expectations of her clients . This inevitably interfered with her ability to run her business and she was unable to earn money to add to her goals. She wasn't discouraged, at least not discouraged for very long. An Investor's Mindset emphasizes resilience—

the ability to learn from mistakes, adapt, and continue moving forward. This component helps young people avoid discouragement and instead view challenges as learning experiences.

As a SPOILED Kid with an Investor's Mindset, our daughter learned about the power of compounding—the idea that small, consistent efforts or investments can lead to big returns over time. This principle applies not just to money but to skills, relationships, and habits as well. Not allowing the setbacks and mistakes to stop her momentum, she kept moving forward to refine her skills, looked up tutorial videos online, and practiced everyday to gain new skills even when we were on vacation or in the evenings after volleyball practice. Through the compounding of her investment of time and efforts, she intuitively knew, would only make her business stronger and more profitable.

Understanding compounding helps kids recognize the value of regular, positive actions and consistent progress. Much like working out one time at the gym over the course of a year doesn't make you as strong as you can be, it takes daily and weekly compounding of exercise, sacrifice, and time to achieve the body goals you have for yourself. Compounding is the path to greater returns. Investing is not only about money—it's also about growing one's skills, character, and relationships. A SPOILED Kid's Investor Mindset focuses on self-improvement and continuous learning. By investing in themselves, they realize that education, experiences, and personal growth are lifelong assets that enrich their lives.

We are so happy to report that our daughter was able to save enough money to achieve her goal of a new phone. Although we still placed constraints on its usage with rules governing a healthy respect for the dangers that can accompany such a device, she felt very proud of herself, and had a profound sense of ownership, responsibility, and accomplishment. She certainly is SPOILED.

An Investor's Mindset equips kids with tools for lifelong success by teaching them to approach life with strategic thinking, resourcefulness, and self-discipline. They learn that investments aren't just about money; they include time, energy, education, and even kindness. By practicing patience, setting meaningful goals, and learning from experience, they understand that wealth includes not only financial gains but also personal fulfillment, resilience, and a sense of purpose. As a parent you can help encourage this mentality in many ways.

Below are just five ways to Cultivate the SPOILED Investor Mindset, but we are sure, as you are becoming a SPOILED Parent, you can think of other creative ways to foster this within your children.

1. Allowances with Goals

Teach kids to allocate their allowance into saving, spending, and giving. Help them set goals for each category to practice purposeful investment.

2. Start Small Investment Projects

Set up a small business project, like a lemonade stand or craft sale, to help them learn about effort, income, costs, and profit. It teaches practical money management and gives them experience with the basics of investing.

3. Family Vision Boards and Planning

Make a family vision board where kids set their goals. Involve them in planning family investments, like a vacation or family purchase, to give them a sense of participation and long-term planning.

4. Celebrate Patience and Growth

When they achieve a long-term goal, celebrate the journey, not just the result. Reinforce the lesson of patience, resilience, and smart decision-making that led them to success.

5. Teach Financial Literacy Early

Use age-appropriate books, games, or digital apps that introduce concepts like saving, budgeting, and investing to make the learning experience engaging.

Investors 4.2:

Our Investment Lesson

When we were looking to purchase our first rental property in Indianapolis, we knew this was more than a financial commitment; it was an investment in our knowledge, our family, and our future. We began by committing time and resources to take a comprehensive class on real estate investing. The class returned more than information; it gave us valuable insights, skills, and a foundational understanding of the industry's complexities. The experience was also invaluable for the connections we made with peers who shared similar goals. Through open exchanges, shared anxieties, and mutual encouragement, we found ourselves bolstered by a network of like-minded individuals, which helped us feel less alone and more empowered in our journey.

Beyond the formal training, we dove into independent research to deepen our understanding of real estate markets and investment strategies. This further exploration gave us a breadth of information, enabling us to make informed, confident decisions. Armed with knowledge, we turned our attention inward and invested in each other. We listened deeply to each other's concerns about potential challenges, discussing how this venture aligned with our beliefs, habits, and philosophies about money's purpose in our lives. These conversations were crucial, transforming what had been a vague idea into a shared vision of manifestation.

Our vision was twofold: to develop multiple income-generating properties that would create a passive income stream for our family and, just as importantly, to set up properties for our daughters by their milestone 16th birthdays. With this clear and meaningful vision, we went a step further to examine its virtue. Could we both believe in it wholeheartedly? Without shared belief, we knew this was an investment we couldn't pursue together. We needed to be aligned in our confidence, commitment, and conviction about this endeavor's merit.

Next, we calculated the value, asking, "Is this investment worth it?" We looked closely at the numbers and opportunity costs—time that might be taken away from our daughters, the energy it would require, and the financial outlay necessary. This assessment of value encompassed both tangible and intangible factors. Was it worth potential family strain? The inevitable stress? Was the financial cost, including the initial purchase, renovations, materials, labor, and contingency funds, justified?

After careful deliberation, we concluded that the

potential returns outweighed the sacrifices. This was a high-value opportunity. So, we activated our volition—our power and agency—to move forward with this choice. We registered with the County Treasurer's Office to participate in the quarterly Tax Sale Auction, giving us a cost-effective entry into the property market. We researched the properties thoroughly, zeroing in on one that fit our goals and strategized for the day of the auction.

When the time came, we were focused and prepared. The auctioneer called our selected property with an opening bid of just $750, the total delinquent taxes owed on the property. We raised our paddle with purpose. In a matter of seconds, the auctioneer's gavel came down, and with it, we had won the property—no counter-bidders, no competition—just $750 for a whole house and land, an investment opportunity that marked an incredible win for us. This was the beginning of our family's empire goals, jumpstarting our path to generational wealth.

This journey not only provided a financial asset but also taught us lessons about patience, unity, and perseverance. As you guide your children to become SPOILED Investors, remember that wealth is multifaceted. It includes experiences, relationships, and knowledge alongside monetary returns. Equip them to live a life of holistic abundance, where every resource is invested with care, and every return, whether financial or personal, builds toward a more fulfilled life.

Always remember that the most valuable things in life rarely come with a price tag. The laughter shared around a dinner table, the conversations that stretch long into the night, the simple presence of the people you love—these are the moments that bring lasting joy and become the foundation you lean on during life's hardest seasons.

Our first real estate investment is a powerful example of that truth. What began as a strategic financial decision—a property purchased with the hope of building wealth—has blossomed into something far more meaningful. Yes, it provided a return on our investment, but the real reward came when we handed the keys to our parents and watched them turn that house into a home.

Now, it's more than just four walls and a roof. It's a gathering place where family stories are told and retold, where grandchildren run through the halls, and where love fills every room. It's a reminder that true wealth isn't measured only in dollars or deeds, but in the memories we create and the legacy we build.

What started as our investment has become Grandma and Grandpa's home—a symbol of love, sacrifice, and the generational roots we are planting. And that transformation is proof that the greatest returns are not always financial; sometimes, they are found in the moments and memories that money could never buy.

INVESTORS 4.3:

The Greatest Investment!

We once came across a profound reflection attributed to the Dalai Lama, where he was asked what surprised him most about humanity and the human experience. His response, as we interpret it, reveals a perspective akin to an investor's mindset. Investors seek opportunities that hold value, retain that value, and yield returns greater than the initial investment. From this lens, the Dalai Lama's observation calls us to consider: what is the greatest investment?

We believe that the most significant investment one can make is in oneself—mind, body, and spirit. You possess inherent and extraordinary value, and without you, little else truly matters. Yet, humanity often places greater value on external acquisitions at the expense of personal well-being. This paradox appears to be what astonished the Dalai Lama most about humanity. He articulated this beautifully:

"Man. Because he sacrifices his health in order to make money. Then he sacrifices money to recuperate his health. And then he is so anxious about the future that he does not enjoy the present; the result being that he does not live in the present or the future; he lives as if he is never going to

die, and then dies having never really lived."

This statement underscores the critical importance of balance and intentionality, values that lie at the heart of the SPOILED Investor framework. A SPOILED Kid is someone who learns to rethink conventional approaches to wealth, time, and purpose. Ironically, it's only after amassing material wealth that many realize the true cost of chasing "things" and money. Until that realization, we are often trapped in the illusion that possessions are the ultimate goal and purpose of life.

Certainly, money can buy comfort, provide a sense of security, and enable access to experiences that bring joy, but it cannot buy happiness itself. You can possess all the wealth in the world, but if your health fails, if you lack meaningful relationships, or if you are dissatisfied with the person you've become in the pursuit of success, then you are not wealthy but profoundly impoverished. As the saying goes: *"Some people are so poor, all they have is money."*

Teach your children that the most valuable investment they can ever make—though not the only one—is in their mind, body, and spirit. These investments form the foundation for everything else in life. To illustrate this concept, we use the analogy of a gallon-sized jug. This jug has a capacity of 8 pints or 4 quarts, but no matter how it is filled, its maximum capacity remains the same—a gallon.

Similarly, we explain to our children that each of us has an internal capacity—a limit to how much we can hold emotionally, mentally, and physically. Life is filled with countless forces competing to fill this internal jug: school, friendships, activities, television, the internet, studying, traveling, relationships, and more. Some of these things, like fleeting trends or shallow pursuits, may quickly evaporate, leaving little lasting fulfillment. Others, such as meaningful relationships, learning, and personal growth, will fill their jug in ways that are deeply enriching and enduring.

We remind them that fulfillment doesn't always mean filling their jug to its maximum capacity. Happiness, peace, or success might only require a portion of their capacity. For instance, they might feel full and content at half-capacity, with the remaining "space" available to hold reserves of love, creativity, and positive energy to pour into others.

However, we emphasize the importance of balance. They must first prioritize their own fulfillment, ensuring their jug is sufficiently filled before they attempt to pour into others. Investing in their well-being—mentally, physically, and spiritually—helps them avoid depletion and ensures they have the energy and resources to support those around them.

By teaching this principle, we instill the understanding that personal investment is not selfish but necessary. It builds stronger individuals who, in turn, can contribute to stronger communities and a better society. When each person invests in themselves, they not only thrive but also have the surplus capacity to lift others without feeling drained. This cycle of self-fulfillment and collective generosity becomes a powerful force for change and connection.

Investors 4.4:

Misplaced Investments

The Dalai Lama's reflection on sacrificing health for wealth, only to later sacrifice wealth to reclaim health, highlights a mindset lacking foresight and balance. This vicious cycle leaves individuals depleted rather than enriched. This is an example of a misplaced investment. The SPOILED Investor framework challenges us to break free from this pattern by promoting intentionality in all forms of investment—not just financial, but also in health, relationships, and time.

When we were younger, there was a widely accepted belief that achieving success required an unrelenting work ethic—a mindset of working tirelessly and sacrificing everything to build your dreams while you were still young. This belief was often glorified through stories of individuals who dedicated 60-80 hours a week to their careers, grinding away and climbing the proverbial "ladder of success." These individuals went above and beyond, volunteering for extra work and taking on endless tasks, often at the expense of family time, self-care, and the opportunity to pause, reflect, recharge, and restore. For many, this was seen as the only path to securing a comfortable future—a way to build their empire and one day retire with financial abundance to enjoy life in their later years. While we certainly respect the value of a strong work ethic, goal setting, and dedication, we also recognize the importance of balance and a more holistic approach to how we invest our time, energy, and resources. We have witnessed countless examples of people who poured their entire lives into their careers, sacrificing their health, family, values, and meaningful experiences in pursuit of financial success. Sadly, when the day of retirement finally arrived, many of them found themselves drained, too tired or unhealthy to fully enjoy the dreams they had spent decades chasing.

Instead of a life filled with the joy they envisioned, they were left with a painful realization: the cost of their financial success had been too high. They had achieved monetary wealth but found themselves impoverished in the areas that matter most—relationships, mental well-being, physical health, spiritual depth, and meaningful life experiences. The years spent chasing monetary riches left them with little to show for it beyond their bank accounts, and they often expressed regret for the misplaced priorities and time they could never get back.

A true SPOILED Investor understands that wealth is far more than financial gain—it is holistic and multifaceted. True wealth encompasses physical health, emotional well-being, spiritual depth, and the richness of human connections. Without these essential elements, financial success alone is hollow and cannot satisfy the deeper needs of the human spirit. A balanced approach to life ensures that the journey to success is as fulfilling as the destination, allowing us to live richly in every sense of the word.

Modeling these foundational values for your children is one of the most powerful investments you can make. Allow them to witness you intentionally caring for your mental, physical, and spiritual well-being. This means showing them what it looks like to prioritize balance, purpose, and intentionality in daily life. For some, this may involve creating sacred family time for heartfelt conversations, engaging in activities that stimulate the mind, and incorporating physical exercises that promote a healthy body.

To remove barriers and ensure our family could fully embrace these values, we made purposeful modifications to our home to foster an environment that supports holistic health and connection. For instance, instead of relying solely on a gym membership, we built a fully functional gym in our home. This allows us to wake up early and do full-body workouts together as a family—eliminating the extra time, resources, and effort required to travel to a gym while encouraging us to stay active.

We also created a theater room that doubles as a game room, where we gather for cozy family movie nights or engage in lively, competitive card and board games. These intentional moments of laughter, competition, and connection strengthen our bond. Additionally, we dedicated space for a meditation room, which serves as a sanctuary for yoga, relaxation, and recharging. Guided meditation and soft music help us start our mornings with positive affirmations and end our evenings by releasing negativity, ensuring we sleep peacefully and begin the next day renewed.

By making thoughtful investments of time, energy, and love into your family, you build what matters most for a lasting legacy: love, relationships, and unity. The return on this investment is immeasurable. We've all heard stories of people who achieved incredible financial wealth but were estranged from their families—often because they spent so much time building monetary wealth that they neglected the people meant to enjoy it with them. While financial stability is undoubtedly an essential component of generational wealth, it should never be the sole focus.

You matter, so prioritize your mental, physical, and emotional health. Your children matter, so be intentional about the time you spend with them—both in quality and quantity. This ensures they grow into adaptable, resilient, and productive individuals. By modeling these values, you'll raise children who understand the true meaning of being SPOILED. This is how you cultivate a legacy that endures for generations.

INVESTORS 4.5:

The Intentional Now

Many of us become so consumed with anxiety about the future that we fail to enjoy the present. This imbalance robs us of a life lived to its fullest, resulting in neither a meaningful present nor a well-prepared future. The present: it is the only reality we can ever truly experience. We can only live in the Now. The past, vast and unchangeable, exists only as a memory—moments once lived in the Now that have since drifted away, never to return. Similarly, the future is not a tangible place but a concept. When we arrive at what we call the future, we discover it is simply another Now, a continuation of this moment. The Now that we inhabit will soon transform into the past, and we, in turn, are living in what our past selves once envisioned as the future. All we have, all we will ever have, is this moment—this precious, fleeting Now.

It is in the Now that our true power lies, where we meet our truest selves. We have the power to invest now, not yesterday for it is forever gone. When we embrace the present with fierce gratitude and unwavering love, we unlock the potential to transform our lives in ways we may never have imagined. The present moment holds the key to aligning with our deepest values, to finding our highest self, and to discovering the boundless potential that resides within each of us. As the saying goes, "*The past is a memory, the future is a mystery, but this moment is a gift. That's why it's called the present.*" By grounding ourselves in the Intentional Now, we realize that we are always exactly where we are meant to be—at the right place, at the right time, doing the right thing.

The concept of an *Intentional Now* refers to consciously engaging with the present moment in a way that aligns with your core values, goals, and intentions. It is the practice of living purposefully in the Now, ensuring that your thoughts, actions, and energy are deliberate and reflective of the life you want to create. Rather than simply reacting to circumstances or drifting through time passively, the Intentional Now is about investing in and taking ownership of your moment-to-moment decisions to bring your higher purpose into focus and practice.

When you are investing in and living in your Intentional Now, it means grounding your present actions in the values that matter most to you. For example, if kindness, integrity, and growth are core values, you approach every interaction or decision with these principles in mind. It's about letting your values shape your behaviors in real time. It is rooted in the awareness of your long-term goals but focuses on what can be done *today* to move toward them. It means understanding that the investment in small, purposeful actions in the present moment—whether it's dedicating time to a project, having an honest conversation, or prioritizing self-care—builds the foundation for future success.

The Intentional Now requires asking yourself, *"Is what I am doing right now in alignment with the person I want to be and the life I want to live?"* It's about choosing actions that are not just convenient or habitual but are thoughtful and intentional steps toward your desired outcomes. Therefore, practicing this involves mindfulness—being fully present and engaged in what you are doing rather than being distracted by the past or future. Whether you're working, spending time with loved ones, or simply resting, the goal is to give your full attention to the task or experience at hand. While it is about purposeful living, it also requires a balance of acceptance and surrender. Life will not always go as planned, and being intentional includes gracefully adjusting your actions and mindset to align with both your goals and the reality of the moment.

When our family is eating dinner together, playing games, or on vacation our Intentional Now turns into action. We value a strong, authentic relationship with our children with family time and understand the finite nature of time. Therefore, we require that we are intentional about putting our devices away, not dwelling on past grievances, rather we engage in real, meaningful conversations during this quality time. By practicing the Intentional Now, it is an opportunity to create a powerful alignment between your actions, values, and goals. This not only ensures that you're living in harmony with your authentic self but also allows you to make measurable progress toward the life you envision for yourself and your children. Over time, the consistency of living intentionally builds habits, fosters deeper connections, and leads to a more meaningful and purpose-driven life.

And by releasing our attachment to the past and our anxiety about the future, we free ourselves from regret, worry, fear, and the other burdens that weigh on the heart. Anchoring ourselves in the present liberates us from the shackles of unworthiness, disharmony, rejection, anger, and the toxic attachments that drain our energy. In this sacred state of presence, we open ourselves to peace, joy, kindness, gratitude, and a profound awareness of the interconnected energy that flows through everything and everyone around us. Being in the present helps us become more present in the lives of those who matter most to us. By centering ourselves in the present, we find the strength to dissolve prejudice, bigotry, addictions, and the false narratives that have kept us small. In this space, we discover self-worth, positive self-esteem, and fulfillment. We tune into the everlasting vibration of love, which is the essence of existence itself, and in doing so, we align with our truest nature.

Remember: life is not waiting for us somewhere down the road. It is happening right here, right now, in the breath we take, the thoughts we think, and the actions we choose. Each moment presents an opportunity to engage with the miracle of existence, to co-create our reality, and to manifest the dreams and desires that align with our higher purpose. By living in the Now, we awaken to the truth that we are not passive participants in life—we are its creators. And every present moment is a chance to choose to live by our values, to embrace gratitude, and to live fully, deeply, and authentically. A SPOILED Investor does not merely save for tomorrow but lives intentionally today, ensuring that every decision—whether financial, personal, or professional—is an investment in both the present and the future.

Investors 4.6:

The $86,400 Investment

The truth is simple yet profound: *we do not have enough time*. When we were young, we often felt invincible, believing that the expanse of life stretched endlessly before us. We were told, "Don't worry, you have plenty of time," and so we postponed dreams, neglected meaningful opportunities, and indulged in the false comfort of having "later." This mindset creates what we call the *"arrogance of time"*—a belief that life is infinite and there will always be time to repair relationships, pursue dreams, or course-correct. Many only come to realize the folly of this thinking when the reality of life's finiteness becomes painfully evident.

While we were living in New York, some friends came to visit. They were very enthusiastic about being a tourist and doing all of the touristy things this great city had to offer. They had a long agenda and only a couple of days. They arrived Wednesday evening and stayed until Sunday evening. It was August. They understood that we all couldn't hang out during the day because work had to take priority on Thursday and Friday, for it was impossible to change the work schedule. Therefore, they were on their own to explore the city while the host was at work. One of the friends had two non-negotiables: he wanted to visit the United Nations and the World Trade Center. We were only able to do one of those and still fulfill the rest of the group's desires. We explored all over the city and had a great time and figured, logistically, it was more convenient to visit the United Nations rather than travel all the way downtown to the World Trade Center and then back uptown for dinner. "Besides," it was stated, "we will have plenty of time to see it next time. It's not like it's going anywhere." One month later, it was gone. While the experience of an office building can now never we had by our friend is not the point, but the arrogance we had in the mindset that we had time.

A SPOILED Investor mindset challenges this arrogance and embraces life's impermanence, fostering a sense of urgency and intentionality. Time is not a limitless resource; it is a fleeting gift. Tomorrow is never promised. Therefore, *the present moment is all we truly have*—a depleting resource that demands our awareness, gratitude, and purposeful action. In New York and as in life we will be confronted with the fact that we do not have time to do everything. But we can make better use of the time we have.

Imagine waking up each morning to find $86,400 deposited into your bank account. What would you do with it? How would you spend it? What portion would you invest to ensure lasting returns, and how much would you allocate for enjoyment, growth, or generosity? If you knew the money would disappear at the end of the day, leaving no opportunity to save or roll it over, you'd likely spend it wisely, with intention and purpose.

Now consider this: each day, you are given 86,400 seconds—the equivalent of 24 hours. Just like the $86,400 in the bank account, these seconds are yours to invest, spend, or waste, but once the day is gone, the "balance" resets, and you cannot reclaim the time. Unlike money, time is a finite, non-renewable resource that cannot be stored for future use or earned back once spent.

Let's break it down a typical day for most people:

- On average, **28,800 seconds (8 hours)** are spent at work.
- Another **3,600 seconds (1 hour)** are spent commuting to and from work.
- Approximately **18,960 seconds (5.25 hours)** are consumed on mobile devices and screens.
- Around **25,200 seconds (7 hours)** are spent sleeping.

This usually leaves just **9,840 seconds (2.75 hours)** each day for the things we say matter most: family, self-care, personal growth, hobbies, and meaningful connections. That's just 11% of our daily time. For many, this small sliver is not spent intentionally but is instead consumed by distractions, leaving even less time for what truly aligns with their values.

Many of us justify this imbalance by telling ourselves, "*One day, I'll have more time.*" We believe the time we spend working and grinding now will buy us the freedom to focus on what matters later. However, time doesn't accumulate like money in a savings account. It's more like a one-way transaction—once it's spent, it's gone forever. Consider this: if you work an average of 8 hours per day, 5 days a week, for 50 weeks a year, you're spending over 7.2 million seconds annually on work. What's the return on that investment, and at what cost to your health, relationships, and happiness? A SPOILED Investor understands that time is the ultimate currency. They intentionally align their time with their values, ensuring every moment spent yields not just financial returns but a life abundant in fulfillment, contribution, and legacy.

The best way to teach your children the value of time is by modeling it yourself. Show them what it looks like to protect, honor, and intentionally invest time in meaningful ways. Teach them not to squander their seconds on distractions, negativity, or unworthy pursuits. Instead, guide them to spend time on:

- **Things that bring meaning and fulfillment.** This could be pursuing their passions, engaging in creative endeavors, or cultivating a spiritual connection. This is also having dedicated, uninterrupted moments to connect with you and their siblings. Whether it's sharing meals, playing games, or having deep conversations, let them see that they are a priority.

- **Activities that offer a return.** Encourage them to invest time in education, skill-building, personal development, and their mental, physical and emotional health. Show your children that taking care of your mental, emotional, and physical health is not a luxury but a necessity. They can achieve this by spending time reading, learning, and improving themselves, demonstrating the importance of lifelong learning and self-care.
- **People who add value.** Teach them the importance of nurturing relationships with those who uplift, inspire, and love them unconditionally. Be mindful of how much time is spent on screens or unproductive habits, and redirect that energy into purposeful actions and positive people.

By teaching your children to view time as their most valuable resource, you are giving them a gift that transcends wealth. When they learn to protect their time, invest it wisely, and live in alignment with their values, they will create lives filled with purpose, joy, and abundance.

Ultimately, the way we spend our time reflects what we truly value. A SPOILED Investor mindset is about ensuring that those 86,400 seconds each day are used to build a life that is not only financially secure but also deeply meaningful. Teach your children to cherish their time, for it is the most precious asset they will ever have.

INVESTORS 4.7:

A Life of True Wealth

True wealth is living a life without regrets, fully immersed in the moment while thoughtfully crafting a legacy for the future. It's about prioritizing the investments that truly matter: the health of your body, the development of your mind, the nurturing of your spirit, and the cultivation of relationships that bring joy and meaning. Through this approach, the *SPOILED Investor framework* empowers individuals to live purposefully, creating a life of balance, intentionality, and holistic wealth.

By embracing these principles, you ensure that, when your time comes, you leave behind a legacy of not just accumulated assets but of a life fully and richly lived. That is the ultimate return on investment when we can help ourselves and our children escape the traps of chasing money at the expense of personal health and close relationships. Instead, we can lead lives marked by balance, purpose, and a legacy that transcends material wealth. In doing so, we not only prepare for the future but also ensure that we are truly present in the moments that matter most.

Achieving financial prosperity often involves building an extensive investment portfolio, but for the **SPOILED Investor**, investing isn't limited to finances alone. There are other powerful areas to invest in: time, energy, love, care, healthy eating habits, exercise, and education. For example, the investment of time in meaningful relationships or the investment of energy in personal development can yield returns that no financial portfolio could replicate. Similarly, the investment of love and care, whether in family, friends, or community, creates bonds and support networks that enrich one's life far beyond material wealth. And education—whether formal or self-driven—is an investment that compounds over a lifetime, enhancing opportunities, refining skills, and fostering adaptability in an ever-changing world.

Making an investment in yourself is one of the best and most rewarding investments you can ever make. Your ability to grow, perform, and lead depends on the daily choices you make to strengthen your mind, body, and spirit. Success in any area of life—whether financial, personal, or professional—starts with self-discipline and intentional habits.

For us, this commitment begins each morning at 5:00 to 5:15 a.m. We have trained ourselves to wake up with purpose, never pressing the snooze button or delaying the start of the day. It's easy to think that an extra nine minutes of sleep won't make much of a difference, but in reality, those nine minutes can quickly multiply into 27 or more minutes, robbing us of valuable time that could be spent on personal development, movement, and mental clarity. Waking up immediately upon hearing the alarm sets the tone for the rest of the day—it forces discipline, prevents sluggishness, and builds mental resilience.

After waking, the first thing we do is hydrate. We drink 8 to 12 ounces of water to jumpstart our system and lubricate our cells. Proper hydration is critical to overall health, affecting everything from brain function to digestion and energy levels. Studies show that dehydration can lead to fatigue, lack of focus, and even mood swings. The general guideline is to drink half of your body weight in ounces of water per day. For example, someone weighing 180 pounds should aim for 90 ounces of water daily to stay properly hydrated. For those who engage in regular physical activity, even more water intake is necessary to replenish fluids lost through sweating.

Fueling our bodies with nutritious foods and being intentional about what we consume is another critical aspect of self-investment. Nutrition is the foundation of our energy, focus, and long-term health. The saying *"You are what you eat"* is not just a cliché—it is a reality that influences everything from our cognitive sharpness to our emotional well-being. Our family prioritizes a balanced diet rich in whole, plant-based foods—lean proteins from plant sources, healthy fats, fiber-rich vegetables, and complex carbohydrates—while eliminating processed foods, artificial additives, and excessive sugar intake.

A well-nourished body leads to enhanced mental clarity, a stronger immune system, improved mood stability, and sustainable energy levels that allow us to fully engage with life's demands. However, our journey toward optimal health was not just about adding more fruits and vegetables to our plates—it was a complete transformation in mindset and lifestyle that began with a single wake-up call.

Our transition to a vegan lifestyle was sparked by a visit to the doctor, where we expected a discussion about genetics after mentioning that our parents had been diagnosed with heart disease, hypertension, and other chronic ailments. Instead, to our surprise, the conversation was not about what we *inherited* in our DNA—it was about what we had been taught to eat.

The doctor explained that while family health histories are often linked to disease, it is not biology that dictates our health outcomes—it is culture, habits, and lifestyle choices. The reason so many families suffer from the same conditions, especially the common non-communicable diseases like heart disease, Type II Diabetes, certain types of cancers, is not necessarily because of genetics but because of the lifestyle choices, foods and eating patterns that are passed down from generation to generation. Our parents likely developed these health issues because of what *their* parents fed them, just as we had been unknowingly following the same nutritional blueprint.

Hearing this shifted our entire perspective. It made us question not just what we were eating but why we were eating it. Were we consuming certain foods because they were truly good for us, or simply because they were familiar, comforting, and ingrained in our culture? This realization led us to extensive research and self-education, which ultimately confirmed what the doctor had said. We had a choice: continue the same patterns and risk the same health issues, or break the cycle and take control of our family's health trajectory.

With this newfound knowledge, we made the bold decision to completely transform our diet and mindset around food. We transitioned to a whole-food, plant-based diet, cutting out all animal products and focusing on consuming nutrient-dense, life-giving foods. It wasn't just about avoiding illness—it was about thriving. We realized that every meal is an opportunity to either fuel disease or fuel vitality, and we chose the latter. And this shift was about more than just food—it was a statement of ownership over our health, our longevity, and our future. We became hyper-intentional about everything we put into our bodies, viewing food as medicine rather than just a means of satisfying cravings.

Since adopting a health-focused, vegan lifestyle, our annual bloodwork has shown remarkable improvements. Our doctor has repeatedly noted that our health markers make it seem as though we are aging in reverse. No longer are we on the trajectory of developing the same chronic conditions that affected our parents and grandparents. Instead, we feel stronger, more energized, and more mentally sharp than ever before. This journey has reinforced a powerful truth: we are not prisoners of our past, nor are we bound by the limitations of culture or tradition. We have the power to rewrite our health story and pass down a legacy of wellness, strength, and longevity to our children.

INVESTORS 4.8:

Investing in Body, Mind, and Future

A healthy body alone is not enough—true wellness is a combination of what we eat, how we think, and what we learn. Alongside our commitment to proper nutrition, we invest just as much energy into cultivating a healthy mindset through reading, continuous education, and self-discipline.

- Reading and Education: Just as we feed our bodies with nutrient-rich foods, we feed our minds with books, research, and thought-provoking discussions that challenge us to grow and evolve.
- Mindset and Discipline: Success in health, finances, and life all require delayed gratification, patience, and intentionality.
- Leading by Example: By living a disciplined, health-conscious, and knowledge-driven lifestyle, we model for our children what it means to truly take ownership of one's well-being.

The shift we made wasn't just about avoiding disease—it was about investing in a future where we are thriving, not just surviving. Our commitment to healthy eating and lifelong learning is a direct reflection of our belief that wealth is more than money—it is the strength of your body, the clarity of your mind, and the power of your choices.

By making these changes, we are ensuring that our children inherit not just financial stability, but the tools, habits, and knowledge necessary to live long, healthy, and fulfilling lives. When our bodies are properly nourished, we think more clearly, work more efficiently, and feel more motivated to pursue our goals. A well-fed body supports an empowered, resilient mind.

Just as we nourish our bodies with healthy food, we also feed our minds with knowledge through daily reading and continuous education. We dedicate time each morning to reading books, listening to podcasts, or engaging with educational material that enhances our financial literacy, leadership skills, and personal development. Expanding our knowledge base keeps us sharp, adaptable, and prepared for opportunities.

Reading regularly strengthens focus, improves cognitive function, and broadens our perspectives. Whether it's books on wealth-building, entrepreneurship, discipline, history, or personal development, we see knowledge as an investment that compounds over time—just like money. Those who consistently read and educate themselves create a mindset of growth, curiosity, and lifelong learning.

By waking up with purpose, staying hydrated, eating healthily, and continuously learning, we ensure that we are operating at our highest potential each day. These investments in ourselves result in:
- Increased productivity and goal achievement
- Higher energy levels and mental sharpness
- Better emotional regulation and resilience
- Stronger physical health and longevity
- The ability to lead by example for our children

When we prioritize self-care and self-discipline, we set the foundation for wealth, success, and generational impact. Being the best version of ourselves allows us to be better parents, spouses, entrepreneurs, and leaders. True success isn't just about accumulating wealth—it's about cultivating the mental, physical, and emotional well-being needed to sustain it.

By making self-investment a daily priority, we ensure that we are prepared to build, sustain, and pass down the SPOILED Mindset to future generations.

Investor 4.9:

Assets and Liabilities

When determining where to focus your investments, it is essential to understand the concept of *value* and the distinction between *assets* and *liabilities*. At its core, an investment is about creating a return—a benefit or gain that exceeds the initial sacrifice. Whether you invest time, energy, or money, the goal is to ensure that what you put in yields something meaningful in return. This understanding is crucial to making sound decisions, particularly in teaching the principles of being a SPOILED Investor.

What Are Assets?

An *asset* is anything that holds or increases in value over time, be it a person, place, thing, or idea. Assets don't just passively exist; they actively contribute to your growth, well-being, or wealth. When you invest in an asset, you are essentially planting a seed that continues to grow and yield benefits, often beyond what you initially sacrificed.

In financial terms, assets can include things like stocks, rental properties, or businesses—anything that generates income or appreciates in value. Beyond finances, assets can also include knowledge, skills, relationships, or even your health. These are the resources that, when nurtured, give back to you in various ways.

Key Characteristics of Assets:
- **Generate Returns**: Assets create value, whether in the form of financial gains, personal growth, or opportunities.
- **Work for You:** Once acquired, an asset continues to provide benefits, sometimes with little ongoing effort.
- **Retain or Appreciate in Value:** Unlike something that diminishes in worth over time, assets either hold their value or grow in it.

Examples of Assets:
- Financial Assets: A rental property that generates monthly passive income.
- Personal Assets: A new skill learned through a course, which can advance your career.
- Relational Assets: Strong connections with mentors or like-minded individuals who inspire and guide you.
- Health as an Asset: Investing in regular exercise and a balanced diet enhances your physical and mental well-being, which can lead to a more productive and fulfilling life.

What Are Liabilities?

While *assets* work for you, growing in value and contributing to your success, **liabilities** do the opposite—they take more than they give, draining your time, energy, and money without providing a meaningful or sustainable return. Recognizing and minimizing liabilities is essential to building financial independence, achieving personal growth, and securing generational wealth.

In financial terms, liabilities are expenses, debts, or obligations that decrease in value or require ongoing payments without generating income. Some common financial liabilities include:

- **Consumer Debt** – Credit card balances for non-essential items, high-interest loans, and payday advances keep you in a cycle of payments without contributing to your wealth.

- **Depreciating Assets** – Unlike real estate or investments, things like new cars lose value over time, making them financial burdens rather than wealth-building tools.

- **Living Beyond Your Means** – Expensive lifestyles that rely on borrowed money rather than earned assets create financial instability, forcing people to work harder just to maintain an illusion of success.

The key to breaking free from financial liabilities is to differentiate between wants and needs, practice delayed gratification, and shift your spending toward investments that yield returns rather than temporary pleasures.

Liabilities are not just financial—they show up in our habits, relationships, and daily decisions. Anything that consistently drains your energy, time, or emotional well-being without adding value to your life is a liability. Some examples include:

- **Unproductive Habits** – Procrastination, excessive social media use, binge-watching TV, and other distractions steal valuable time that could be used for self-improvement or wealth-building activities.

- **Toxic Relationships** – Surrounding yourself with negative, unsupportive, or manipulative people can drain your energy and confidence, preventing you from reaching your full potential.

- **Unhealthy Lifestyles** – Poor diet, lack of exercise, and sleep deprivation take a toll on your body and mind, ultimately leading to medical expenses and lower productivity.

- **Fear-Based Thinking** – A mindset of scarcity, self-doubt, or complacency can hold you back from taking risks, pursuing opportunities, and achieving financial independence.

Recognizing your liabilities is the first step, but the real power lies in converting them into assets. Here's how:

- **Replace Consumer Debt with Investments** – Instead of spending on unnecessary items, put money into assets like savings, stocks, or business ventures that grow over time.

- **Swap Time-Wasting Habits for Growth Activities** – Trade mindless scrolling for reading, learning, or developing a new skill that increases your value.

- **Upgrade Your Circle** – Surround yourself with people who challenge, inspire, and support your growth, replacing toxic relationships with meaningful connections.

- **Prioritize Health and Well-Being** – Invest in nutritious food, exercise, and mental wellness, ensuring that you have the energy and longevity to build wealth and enjoy it.

By consistently evaluating whether something is helping or hindering your progress, you begin shifting from a liability-driven lifestyle to one focused on assets, growth, and long-term success. Every decision—whether financial, personal, or emotional—should be made with one question in mind:

"**Does this add value to my life, or does it take away from it?**"

When our family put this way of thinking into practice, we generally ask a variation of these questions to ourselves and then seek input from each other when confronted with a decision rather financial, personal, or family related:
- What's the Return? Will this investment give back to you, and how?
  - For example, is a college education an asset? Yes, if it leads to career opportunities or personal growth that outweighs its cost.
- Is It Depreciating or Appreciating? Will this hold or grow in value, or will it diminish over time?
  - For instance, is a car an asset? Only if it's used for income (like ride-sharing or deliveries). Otherwise, it's a liability.
- Does It Work for Us or will we have to work for it? Will this investment make your life easier, more fulfilling, or more prosperous?
  - A small business could be an asset if it generates income, but if it requires endless work with no profit, it becomes a liability.

Helping kids focus on assets rather than liabilities creates a foundation for financial stability, personal growth, and a fulfilling life. When they understand that assets are tools that help them work smarter, not harder, they begin to see life through a lens of opportunity. Liabilities, while sometimes necessary, should always be evaluated critically to ensure they don't overshadow the pursuit of sustainable growth.

How to Teach Kids About Assets vs. Liabilities

Real-Life Examples: Show your children tangible examples of assets and liabilities in your daily life. For instance, explain why saving for a family vacation (a short-term liability) can bring value through shared experiences but buying unnecessary items on credit leads to financial strain.

Engage in Conversations: Talk about decisions they make with their money, time, or energy. For example, discuss how learning a new skill can be an asset for their future.

Practice Decision-Making: Give your children scenarios to evaluate. Ask them if something is an asset or liability and why. Help them think critically about what will provide the most value.

Track Value Together: Start a project where they can see the growth of an asset. For instance, give them a small amount of money to invest in a business idea or savings account. Let them see how it grows over time.

Highlight Hidden Assets: Teach them that assets aren't always tangible. A good reputation, a strong work ethic, or emotional resilience are intangible assets that pay dividends throughout life.

When we learn how to identify and eliminate liabilities, you gain financial freedom, mental clarity, and personal empowerment, creating a life built on assets that will sustain us and future generations. By teaching the value of assets and the dangers of liabilities early, you set your children up to become **SPOILED Investors**—individuals who know how to make decisions that lead to lasting wealth and happiness.

Investors 4.10:

The Asset Mindset

An Asset Mindset is the ability to view every action, decision, and relationship as an investment—one that can generate returns in the form of knowledge, opportunities, financial growth, and personal development. It is the foundation of true wealth-building, not just in terms of money, but in the cultivation of skills, relationships, health, and wisdom that will continue to pay dividends over time.

Too often, people think of assets only in the financial sense—stocks, real estate, businesses—but the greatest assets are not just things you own; they are things you cultivate within yourself. Your knowledge, time, relationships, reputation, and even your mindset itself are all powerful assets that can appreciate in value if nurtured correctly.

Consider every action you take as an opportunity to invest in something that gives back. If you invest time in learning about entrepreneurship, finance, or leadership, the knowledge gained becomes an asset that opens doors to new opportunities, income streams, and career advancements. If you invest in your health, your energy levels, mental clarity, and longevity increase, allowing you to be more effective in every aspect of life.

Your ability to learn, adapt, and grow is an asset that compounds over time. The more you read, the more you know. The more you know, the more you can apply. The more you apply, the more valuable you become—not just to yourself but to your family, your community, and the generations that follow.

Understanding that you yourself are an asset is one of the most crucial realizations on the path to generational wealth. Your mind, your love, your care, your discipline, and your very life are all part of the legacy you are building. When you see yourself as an asset, you begin to operate differently—you start to move with intention, seek wisdom, prioritize growth, and protect your value.

It is essential to teach your children that they, too, are valuable assets with limitless potential. Every experience they embrace, every skill they develop, and every healthy habit they form increases their worth—not just in financial terms, but in character, wisdom, and ability. When children grow up with an Asset Mindset, they stop seeing themselves as passive participants in life and start seeing themselves as active investors in their future.

- **Encourage Learning as an Investment** – Teach your children that every book they read, every problem they solve, and every lesson they absorb **increases their value and capabilities.**

- **Promote Healthy Living as an Asset** – Show them that their body and mind are the foundation of their future success and that taking care of themselves is a powerful investment.

- **Help Them Build Strong Relationships** – Teach them that relationships are social capital, and that positive connections with people who uplift and inspire them will yield lifelong rewards.

- **Instill Financial Intelligence** – Show them the power of delayed gratification, smart investing, and wealth-building habits, so they understand how money can work for them instead of the other way around.

An Asset Mindset is not just about acquiring resources; it's about knowing how to extract value from every person, situation, and experience. Even in setbacks, there is something to be gained—a lesson, a new strategy, a deeper resilience. When you train yourself to seek the value in everything, you turn every moment into an opportunity for growth.

For example, a failed business venture is not a loss—it is an education. A difficult relationship is not a burden—it is a lesson in patience, communication, and boundaries. Even in moments of hardship, those who possess an Asset Mindset do not dwell in frustration; they extract wisdom, adjust their approach, and continue moving forward.

The goal of wealth-building is not simply to accumulate material things but to create systems, knowledge, and habits that will sustain and uplift future generations. Those who master an Asset Mindset understand that wealth is about more than money—it is about freedom, wisdom, health, and the ability to make an impact.

By instilling this mindset in yourself and your children, you break cycles of scarcity and reactionary living. You shift from consuming to creating, from surviving to thriving, from being controlled by circumstances to designing your own future.

So, ask yourself daily:
- Am I treating myself as an asset?
- Am I making decisions that increase my value?
- Am I instilling an Asset Mindset in my children?
- Am I seeking opportunities to grow in every experience?

When you embrace an Asset Mindset, every step you take moves you and your family closer to generational wealth, personal empowerment, and a legacy that lasts.

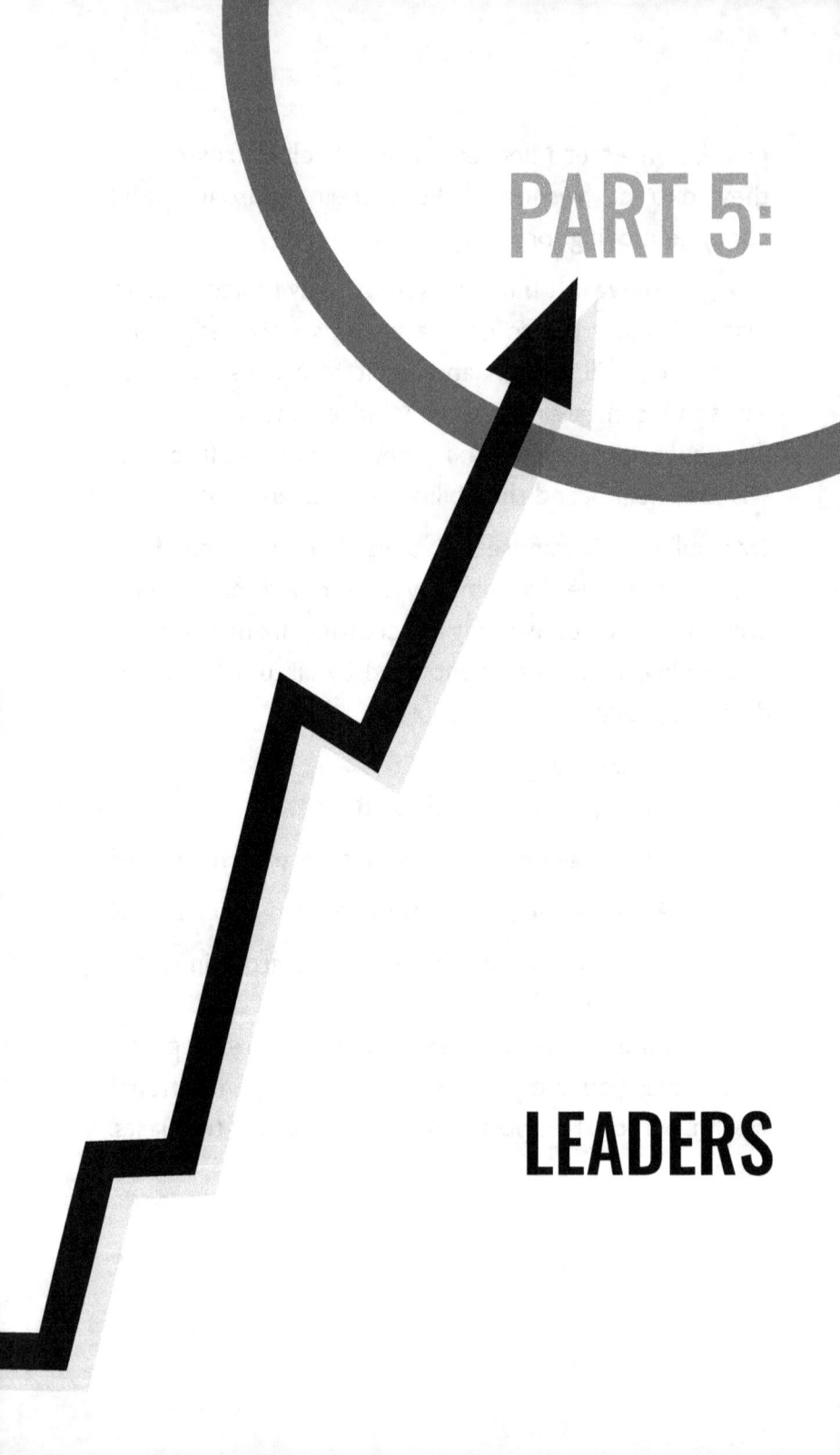

SPOILED Leadership is both a privilege and a challenge, varying greatly depending on the context—whether in parenting, education, advocacy, entrepreneurship, or navigating professional and social spaces. Each situation demands a unique approach, but the foundation of effective leadership remains consistent: a mindset rooted in creating, serving, and improving the quality of life for others. True leadership isn't about authority, position, or prestige; it's about purpose, responsibility, and the ability to inspire and cultivate growth in those around us.

Before we could effectively teach our children the meaning of leadership, we first had to learn it and embody it ourselves. Leadership isn't an innate trait that automatically develops upon becoming a parent, mentor, or business owner. It is a skill honed through intentionality, reflection, and action. We had to recognize that leadership isn't defined by a title—it's defined by the consistency of our actions, the integrity of our decisions, and the impact we have on those we guide. Leadership is relational and purposeful. It requires us to not only direct but also to listen, not only to instruct but also to model, and not only to support but also to challenge.

Leadership is often framed as a role of influence, direction, and decision-making, but at its core, it is a mindset—one that determines whether a leader is truly effective in inspiring and empowering others. A self-serving, inward-focused leader may appear strong in their authority, but they lack the trust, collaboration, and innovation that define great leadership. An outward mindset, as described by thought leaders and researchers, shifts the focus from personal ambition to recognizing and addressing the needs, challenges, and potential of those we lead. This approach transforms leadership from a position of control to an endeavor of service, growth, and collaboration.

As SPOILED parents—committed to raising Savers, Producers, Owners, Investors, Leaders, Entrepreneurs, and Disciplined individuals—we understood that fostering leadership in our children required more than discipline and direction. It meant cultivating environments where they could develop self-awareness, resilience, and confidence. It required us to truly hear them, assess their individual needs, and equip them with critical thinking skills, problem-solving abilities, and the tools of self-advocacy. Leadership in parenthood isn't about controlling outcomes but about preparing our children to navigate their own paths with wisdom, courage, and purpose.

We teach our children that leadership is not about popularity, power, or prestige—it's about standing boldly for what is right, even when it's uncomfortable. It means amplifying voices that need to be heard, confronting injustice, and actively working to create meaningful change for individuals and communities. Leaders are not just loud; they are strategic, persistent, and guided by an unwavering commitment to fairness and equity.

SPOILED Leadership means raising children who take ownership of their futures—not waiting for opportunities but creating them. They learn that leadership requires making difficult decisions, holding themselves accountable, and understanding that challenges are not roadblocks but stepping stones. They develop the ability to navigate setbacks with resilience, seeing every failure as a lesson and every success as an opportunity to lift others.

Beyond the home, leadership in professional spaces is about balancing empathy with accountability, vision with execution, and long-term growth with immediate needs. Whether guiding a team, leading an organization, or mentoring individuals, effective leadership demands adaptability, integrity, and the ability to inspire others toward a shared purpose. It's about fostering a culture of excellence and ensuring that every voice is valued. It also involves encouraging people to stretch beyond their comfort zones to reach their full potential. A SPOILED Leader does not operate in isolation but builds ecosystems of support and empowerment. They recognize that leadership is not about personal gain but about leaving a lasting impact. They understand that sustainable success is achieved not through individual brilliance but through collaboration, shared vision, and the collective growth of those around them.

Ultimately, great leadership is about being adaptable while staying anchored to a core purpose: empowering others, fostering growth, and making decisions that uplift and inspire. SPOILED Leadership is a mindset about ownership—not just of businesses or wealth, but of responsibilities, values, and the impact we have on the world around us.

SPOILED Leaders must be intentional in their actions, disciplined in their approach, and unwavering in their pursuit of excellence. Whether in parenting, business, community work, or professional leadership, they embrace challenges as opportunities to grow and inspire others to do the same. What we want to stress is Leadership isn't just a title. It's not about who's loudest, tallest, oldest, or always right. Leadership is a mindset. It's a way of thinking, acting, and caring about the people and the world around you. And in the SPOILED family, leadership isn't optional—it's essential.

Our goal as parents isn't to raise followers who wait for someone else to decide. Our job is to raise Leaders—SPOILED kids who lead with wisdom, courage, and compassion. But leadership takes many forms. And great leaders know which form to use, depending on the moment, the mission, and the people involved.

Let's explore five powerful types of leadership every SPOILED kid (and parent) should understand: Outward-minded Leadership, Situational Leadership, Servant Leadership, Transformational Leadership, and the visionary mindset that drives them all forward.

When we embrace leadership as a commitment to service, progress, and empowerment, we don't just lead—we transform. We create a legacy of strength, wisdom, and purpose that extends far beyond ourselves, shaping the next generation of leaders who will carry our vision forward.

Leaders 5.1:

Outward Leadership

An inward mindset in leadership distorts a leader's perception of those around them, reducing people to mere obstacles, tools, or irrelevant factors in the pursuit of personal or organizational success. Leaders operating from this perspective may unconsciously prioritize their own ambitions, often becoming so consumed by their objectives that they fail to recognize or acknowledge the needs, contributions, and struggles of their team members. This self-focused approach can breed environments of competition rather than collaboration, where individuals feel undervalued, unheard, or even expendable.

The consequences of an inward mindset manifest in various detrimental ways. Leaders who see others as obstacles may resort to defensive leadership, resisting differing perspectives and dismissing constructive feedback. When people are viewed as tools, leaders may exploit their skills without investing in their development, leading to burnout and disengagement. In cases where individuals are deemed irrelevant, leaders may overlook key voices, stifling innovation and inclusivity within the team.

Practically, this mindset often results in micromanagement, as leaders struggle to trust others to take ownership of tasks. A lack of delegation not only stifles creativity and autonomy but also signals a fundamental distrust in the capabilities of the team. Furthermore, an inward mindset fosters disengagement from team dynamics—leaders may become isolated in decision-making, disregarding input from those closest to the work. Over time, this erodes morale, weakens relationships, and reduces overall organizational effectiveness.

Ultimately, an inward-focused leader operates in a silo, unaware of the ripple effects of their choices. Their leadership, instead of being a force for empowerment, becomes a barrier to growth—both for themselves and those they lead.

Conversely, an outward mindset recognizes that leadership is fundamentally relational, not merely transactional. Rather than viewing leadership as a means to extract performance or compliance, leaders with an outward focus see their role as one of service, empowerment, and shared success. They understand that sustainable achievement is not an individual endeavor but a collective effort, where each person's contributions, challenges, and aspirations matter.

Leaders who embrace an outward mindset cultivate environments where people feel valued, heard, and equipped to perform at their best. They prioritize creating a culture of trust, psychological safety, and mutual respect, understanding that when people feel genuinely supported, they are more engaged, innovative, and willing to take initiative. This leadership approach requires a fundamental shift in thinking—one that moves beyond self-interest and positional authority toward a deep commitment to the growth and well-being of others.

At the core of an outward mindset are three essential qualities: deep listening, empathy, and perspective-taking. Deep listening goes beyond merely hearing words; it involves actively seeking to understand the emotions, motivations, and concerns behind what is being said. Empathy allows leaders to connect with the experiences of others, acknowledging their struggles and aspirations in a way that fosters genuine relationships. Perspective-taking ensures that leaders do not operate from a narrow, self-centered viewpoint but instead consider how their decisions impact others, both immediately and in the long term.

This outward shift transforms leadership from control-based management into an endeavor of meaningful influence. Leaders become facilitators of growth, ensuring that individuals not only accomplish tasks but also develop their own leadership capacities. The result is a thriving team or organization where collaboration replaces competition, innovation flourishes, and collective success is not just an ideal but a lived reality.

Key Aspects of an Outward Mindset in Leadership

1. Seeing People as People

    Leadership with an outward mindset starts by seeing individuals not as employees, subordinates, or stakeholders, but as people with their own needs, aspirations, and concerns. This perspective fosters mutual respect and trust, which are critical for engagement and motivation.

2. Creating a Culture of Accountability

    Leaders with an outward mindset take responsibility not just for their actions but also for how their leadership affects others. Instead of blaming teams for failures, they assess whether they have provided the right tools, vision, and support necessary for success.

3. Empowering Others to Lead

    True leadership is not about hoarding power but about distributing it. An outward-minded leader creates opportunities for others to step up, contribute, and take ownership. They recognize that leadership is not about control but about enabling people to unlock their potential.

4. Adaptability and Continuous Growth

    Organizations and teams thrive when leaders

remain adaptable, recognizing that growth comes from being open to feedback and willing to change. An outward-minded leader actively seeks to learn from those they lead, ensuring that leadership is a dynamic and evolving process.

5. Serving the Greater Good

    Beyond individual and organizational success, an outward mindset in leadership considers the broader impact on communities, industries, and future generations. Ethical decision-making, equity, and sustainability become guiding principles rather than afterthoughts.

Leaders who embrace an outward mindset create situations and communities where trust, collaboration, and shared vision drive progress. Employees feel valued, teams perform at higher levels, and organizations become places of innovation and impact. More importantly, outward-minded leadership fosters resilience and adaptability—qualities necessary in an ever-changing world.

In essence, leadership as an outward mindset endeavor is about recognizing that success is not a solo journey. It is the result of lifting others, aligning with a shared purpose, and leading with a heart that sees, hears, and serves.

LEADERS 5.2:

Situational Leadership

Leadership isn't a one-size-fits-all kind of thing. That's one of the first truths every great leader must learn. There isn't a magic formula or fixed way to lead, especially not when it comes to parenting. Real leadership—especially the kind required to raise SPOILED Kids—requires wisdom, awareness, and the ability to adjust. That's what **Situational Leadership** is all about.

As parents, we carry the incredible responsibility of guiding our children's growth and development. But no two seasons of childhood are the same. What worked last year might not work today. And what worked for one child may not work for another. Leadership in the family means paying attention to what *this moment* requires—and responding accordingly.

The Copycat Stage

In the earliest years of parenting, we are our children's entire world. They watch everything we do, listen to every word we say, and mirror our mannerisms, our tone, our habits, and even our moods. We call this the *Copycat Stage*—a critical developmental phase when children learn most by imitating the adults in their lives.

During this time, it's not about what we teach. It's about what they catch. Think about it: we didn't formally teach our children to speak English. We spoke it around them. Their brilliant, sponge-like brains absorbed it. They learned sentence structure, emotion, humor, and meaning by copying what they heard and saw. Even the speed in which they speak or the sounds that words make, referred to as accents, come from the copying the way we do things with language.

That same dynamic plays out with beliefs, values, and behaviors. If we want our children to speak kindness, they must *hear* it from us first. If we want them to act with discipline, they must *see* it modeled. If we want them to believe in themselves, they must *feel* believed in.

So the question for us, as parents, becomes: *What are our children catching from us?* Are they picking up patience or panic? Generosity or judgment? Respect or rigidity? Situational leadership at this stage means modeling what we want to multiply. It means living the values we want to pass on to future generations.

The Counseling Stage

Then comes a shift—a moment every parent recognizes but few are truly ready for, they stop doing and copying everything we do the way we do them.

It's the time in their lives when our kids begin to ask, "Why?"

Why do we do it this way? Why can't I go there? Why do I have to follow this rule?

This marks the beginning of the *Counseling Stage*, when your child is no longer satisfied with simply copying you. They want to understand you. They want to understand the world. They're forming their own beliefs and testing boundaries, not out of defiance, but from a deep desire to make sense of their environment.

This is a sacred stage—one that many parents accidentally miss by shutting down curiosity with phrases like, "Because I said so," or "That's just how it is." But Situational Leadership tells us to pause. To listen. To lean in. When children ask questions, it's not rebellion—it's trust. They're coming to you because they *believe* you have wisdom worth sharing. And if we respond with patience, love, and honesty—even when we don't know the answer—we strengthen that trust.

Sometimes the best answer is, "That's a great question. Let's find out together." In doing so, we teach our children *how* to think, not just *what* to think. We teach them how to seek truth, how to navigate complexity, and how to respect different perspectives.

That's not just leadership. That's love.

Coaching Stage and the Game of Life

Eventually, the questions give way to actions.

Our children step onto the court of life, and we shift once again—this time into **the Coaching Stage**.

Coaches don't play the game for the team. They equip. They teach. They prepare. And when it's game time, they move to the sidelines—not because they've stopped caring, but because they've done their job.

We remember coaching our daughters' basketball team. At first, we had to teach the fundamentals: how to dribble, shoot, pass, and work together. They copied us, then asked questions to understand the game. But when it was time to play, we couldn't be on the court with them. We had to trust in what we taught that they would execute to the best of their abilities, and continue to help them by drawing up plays from the bench.

Parenting is much the same. Our job is not to play *for* our children but to prepare them so they can play *well* on their own. That's hard for many of us. We want to prevent the turnovers. We want to stop them from missing the shot. We want to remove the defense. We want to take the collisions for them. But if we always intercept the ball, they never learn how to handle it themselves.

When your child fails a test, falls out with a friend, or faces something hard—you may want to fix it all. But Situational Leadership reminds us: this is their moment to grow. You're still the coach, still on the sidelines, ready to support—but now is the time for them to *play*. And when they foul? They'll return to the bench. They'll sit beside you. That's when you guide them, counsel them, and remind them of who they are and how to move forward. The trust built in those earlier stages—Copying and Counseling—makes the Coaching Stage strong.

Cheerleading Stage

And then there are moments when what they need most from you is not instruction or correction—but encouragement. That's when we become *Cheerleaders*.

When our daughter missed a shot, we'd yell, "Shake it off! Get back on defense! That play is over!" And when she nailed the layup? We'd cheer just as loudly, echoing our excitement throughout the gym—and still remind her: "Get back on defense! That play is over. The game's not done yet."

Why? Because parenting through a Situational Leadership lens means keeping them grounded. Not too high when they win, not too low when they lose. Just steady, focused, and encouraged every step of the way.

Cheerleading isn't passive. It's powerful. It tells your child: "I see you. I believe in you. I'm proud of you." Those words matter. They echo. They become the soundtrack playing in their minds when life gets loud.

Situational Leadership is the art of reading the moment—and responding with the right energy. Sometimes we lead by example (Copycat Stage). Sometimes by answering questions (Counseling Stage). Sometimes by preparing and trusting (Coaching Stage). And sometimes by shouting encouragement from the stands (Cheerleading Stage).

This type of leadership builds flexibility, empathy, and emotional intelligence. It helps children feel seen, supported, and safe—and that makes all the difference.

So, parents, ask yourselves:
- When was the last time you adjusted your leadership style based on your child's emotional or developmental need?
- Are you trying to coach when they need counseling? Are you giving commands when they just need to copy?
- Are you standing in the game when it's time to let them play—and be ready to cheer instead?

And have your SPOILED Kids think about this too:
- Have you ever helped a friend who was struggling, not by telling them what to do, but by just being there?
- Can you recall a time when your support mattered more than your solution?

Situational Leadership means having the heart to care and the wisdom to adapt. It means knowing when to step in and when to step back. And when we practice it at home, we equip our children to practice it everywhere. In the end, leadership isn't about control. It's about connection. And when we connect with our children in the way they need *right now*, we help them become leaders who will do the same for others—for life. For this game called Life.

Leaders 5.3:

Servant Leadership

Of all the leadership styles we teach in the journey of raising SPOILED Kids, perhaps none is more misunderstood—or more powerful—than Servant Leadership. When we hear the word *"leader"*, we often picture someone out front: loud, confident, pointing the way. Maybe they're holding a clipboard, making decisions, setting deadlines, or commanding a room. That kind of leadership is real—but it's not the only kind. And it's certainly not the only kind that matters.

Servant Leadership flips the script. Instead of asking, *How do I get ahead?*, a Servant Leader asks, *How can I help others rise?* It may sound backward at first. After all, isn't the leader supposed to be the boss? The one giving orders? But in truth, the greatest leaders in history—those who made the most lasting impact—weren't the ones demanding attention. They were the ones giving support.

We can recall a time when our youngest daughter came home unusually quiet. Not the kind of quiet that means she was tired from a long day, but the kind that holds something heavy in the heart. We gently asked what was wrong. With a soft voice, she told us about a moment that had unfolded in her classroom that day. A classmate—a second-grader just like her—was being teased. Not for how she dressed or how she spoke, but for her *faith*. The student was practicing a religious fast, abstaining from food and drinking during specific hours of the day. As part of her devotion, she also chose to spend recess quietly, away from gossip and the noise of playground drama.

But in the eyes of some of her classmates, this set her apart. It made her "weird." "Different." An easy target. So, there she sat during recess—alone by the fence, head down, eyes filled with tears, trying her best to hold on to her spiritual discipline while being pulled apart by peer judgment. And that's when our daughter did something that stopped *us* in our tracks.

She walked away from the game she was playing—the giggles, the friends, the fun—and sat down beside the crying girl. No announcement. No performance. No, "Look at me, being a helper." Just presence. Just care. Just love in action.

She didn't say much. She didn't need to. Sometimes leadership doesn't look like giving orders or standing at the front of the line. Sometimes it looks like *sitting beside someone who's hurting*, saying with your presence, *You're not alone.*

Later that night, she quietly asked us not to pack her lunch for the rest of the week. We raised our eyebrows.

"Why?" we asked.

"I want to fast with her," she said. "So she doesn't feel alone."

We parents are usually unprepared for that kind of moment. At least we were. We were humbled, inspired—and honestly, we were learning from *her*.

But it didn't stop there. A few days later, other parents reached out to us. Their children had come home talking about what our daughter had done. Some of them had asked if they, too, could try fasting—not because they were joining the same religion, but because they wanted to show support, compassion, and solidarity. One simple act of empathy spread like wildfire—not loud, not flashy, but *deep*. That is the heart of Servant Leadership.

Servant Leadership isn't about taking the spotlight. It's about seeing someone else's needs—and moving to meet them. It's not necessarily rooted in authority from others, but in the compassion and permission you grant to yourself. Servant Leaders operate from a place of humility, empathy, and responsibility. They don't seek power for themselves—they use their power to lift others.

They ask questions like: What does my teammate need to do their best? How can I make things better for someone else? Is there someone being left out or overlooked that I can include? Can I help without needing recognition? How can I support someone today? Who around me might be struggling silently? What can I give without expecting something in return?

You can teach your SPOILED Kids that they don't need to be the class president or team captain to lead. They don't need a loud voice to make a big impact. All they need is *heart*—and the courage to act on it. Our children are learning from us, but they're also *teaching* us. Our daughter taught us a powerful truth that day: Sometimes, the greatest kind of leadership doesn't stand above—it *kneels beside*. And in doing so, it lifts *everyone* higher.

Are we modeling Servant Leadership? Are we showing our kids how to use their time, energy, and influence to help someone else rise? Are we sitting beside people in their quiet moments—not just cheering them on in their victories?

Sometimes, it's as simple as cleaning up a shared space without being asked. Other times, it's about defending someone who's being picked on or giving credit to others instead of taking it for yourself. This type of leadership might not look flashy. You might not get a round of applause. But the impact is deep—and lasting.

Modeling Servant Leadership at Home

For SPOILED Parents, raising a Servant Leader begins with modeling. Our children are always watching.

They see how we treat waitstaff at a restaurant. They notice whether we hold the door open for someone behind us. They pick up on how we speak about others when no one's listening. They are listening to how we deal with the less fortunate, do we scoff at the person experiencing homelessness, or are we kind? When they witness the way we serve others they will look for that kind of service for themselves. And here's a secret: when children feel *served* by their parents—not controlled, but supported—they learn how to serve others from a place of wholeness, not obligation.

Here are a few ways we can model Servant Leadership at home:

- **Do the small things with great love.** Whether it's folding laundry, packing lunches, or listening without interruption, we show our kids what it means to serve quietly and consistently.
- **Talk about "we" instead of "me."** In conversations, shift the focus from personal success to shared success. Celebrate your family's victories as a team.
- **Recognize and reward kindness.** When your child does something generous or helpful, name it. Call it out. Let them know that those moments *are* leadership.
- **Serve them by seeing them.** Truly seeing your child—acknowledging their feelings,

validating their experiences, and showing up with patience—teaches them to do the same for others.

If we want our kids to grow up valuing service, we must show them that *serving others is not a weakness—it's strength in action.* Many kids (and adults) confuse service with weakness. "If I'm always helping others, won't people walk all over me?" they might wonder.

But true service is not about shrinking—it's about standing tall and offering your strength to someone who needs it. Servant Leaders are grounded. They know their worth. They don't serve from a place of guilt or fear—they serve because they *can.*

In fact, some of the most influential leaders of all time—Dr. Martin Luther King Jr., Mother Teresa, Nelson Mandela—led through service. They didn't seek power for power's sake. They used their influence to build bridges, heal wounds, and raise others up.

Their leadership wasn't loud, but it was unshakable. Their names are remembered not because they stood above others—but because they stood for others.

So whether you're a kid learning how to lead at school or a parent modeling leadership at home, remember this: Servant Leadership isn't about being in charge—it's about being in service. It's not about who's at the front of the line. It's about who's willing to *step aside* and let someone else shine. It's not about being seen. It's about *seeing*.

At the heart of raising SPOILED Kids is this idea: *We don't raise bosses. We raise builders—of character, compassion, and community.* For your SPOILED Kids, here's the truth: Real leadership doesn't always look like a megaphone. It might look like sharing your lunch with someone who forgot theirs. It may look like sitting with the new student who hasn't made friends yet. It could be picking up trash that you didn't drop. It is encouraging your sibling when they're frustrated or standing up for someone who's being treated unfairly. Those moments matter. They're not small—they're seeds. And each time you act with kindness, you're planting the kind of leadership of which this world needs more.

Reflection for Parents:

When was the last time your child saw you serve without needing to be seen? What's one way you can model quiet leadership in your family this week?

Reflection for SPOILED Kids:

Think about someone at school, on your team, or in your family who could use a little extra help or kindness. What could you do—without being asked—to show you care?

LEADERS 5.4:

Transformational Leadership

Some leaders manage. Some leaders maintain. But **Transformational Leaders?** They *inspire*. They *elevate*. They *change the game*—not just for themselves, but for the people around them.

Transformational leadership is more than doing a good job or being responsible. It's about creating a *vision* for what could be, and then working with others to make that vision real. Transformational leaders make things better, not just for today—but for tomorrow. Transformational Leaders light sparks in people. They challenge others to grow. And most importantly—they grow, too. They don't settle for the way things *have always been*. They ask:

- What if we tried something different?
- How can I help others believe in themselves?
- What can we build that wasn't here before?

One afternoon, we were sitting around the kitchen table with our daughters. They had been talking about how their school didn't have any kind of reward system that celebrated *kindness*. You could get praised for good grades or athletic skills, but what about the kid who helps others every day without being asked?

Or the student who notices when someone is feeling left out? That night, one of our daughters came to us with an idea:

"What if we made a 'Kindness Tree' at school? Every time someone sees an act of kindness, they can write it down on a paper leaf and add it to the tree. By the end of the month, the tree would be full—and everyone would see how much kindness really happens around here." That's Transformational Leadership.

She saw a need. She imagined something new. She inspired action. And then she got to work—talking to her teacher, rallying friends, creating a system. That one idea turned into a school-wide project that changed the culture of her classroom. This was the catalyst for publishing the book, *Orange* (Slack, D. 2020. Know Wonder Publishing.), which helps children learn to be more kind, understanding their worth, and their power to make positive, transformational change in the lives of others.

This is what happens when kids are given room to lead with heart and vision. They don't just follow rules—they *reshape realities*.

Four Pillars of Transformational Leadership

Parents and kids alike can grow into transformational leaders by living out these four essential traits:

1. **Vision** – They see the big picture and help others imagine it too. Vision isn't about being perfect—it's about believing in possibility.
2. **Inspiration** – They use their words and actions to encourage others. They help people see what's great about themselves, even when they can't see it yet.
3. **Growth Mindset** – They believe people can change. They offer support, feedback, and second chances.
4. **Courage to Challenge** – They speak up when something is wrong and lead the way toward what's right, even when it's not easy.

Transformational leaders don't just want to "win"—they want everyone to rise. Parents, here's where we play a major role. Kids don't become transformational leaders if they're always told to sit still, follow rules, and not ask questions. We must encourage our children to be bold thinkers and brave doers. That means teaching them to think critically—asking questions, making connections, and not just accepting things as they are. It means empowering them to challenge injustice when they see it, to speak up when something isn't working, and to believe their voice matters. Most of all, we must create space for them to dream out loud—because their ideas, their hopes, and their visions for a better world are the blueprints for the future we all need.

Of course, this can be hard. Sometimes transformational leadership shows up as rebellion or resistance. Your child might start asking *why* a lot more. They may push back on family traditions, school routines, or community norms. When that happens, don't shut them down—*lean in*. Help them shape their thoughts. Ask them questions. Listen with curiosity, not correction.

We have made a conscious decision that we are not raising robots. We are raising revolutionaries in the best sense—kids who are bold enough to reimagine the world, and kind enough to include others in the process. One action can spark a movement.

Ultimately, our SPOILED Kids are becoming not just leaders but legacy-makers. They don't just lead for today—they leave footprints that others can follow tomorrow. This is the essence of all that we desire to instill within our children: the concept of doing now what will last for generations to come. To secure a positive future for themselves, their children, and the society at large. When you teach your children to be transformational, you're teaching them to be architects of a better world.

And when you show them how to take a good situation and make it *great*, or to take a broken system and make it *whole*, you're handing them the keys to leadership that outlasts a moment—it shapes a generation.

Reflection for Parents:

Are there places in your family or community where your child might be ready to lead positive change? How can you support that growth—even if it makes you a little uncomfortable?

Reflection for SPOILED Kids:

Is there something around you—at school, in your friend group, or at home—that could be better? What's one step you could take to start making that change today?

Leaders 5.5:

Visionary Leadership

There is a special kind of leader that doesn't just respond to what *is*—they dream about what *could be*. These are Visionaries. Kids are natural visionaries. Have you ever heard your child describe their ideas for the future? "I'm going to be a vet and a lawyer and build a rocket ship and open a bakery for dogs!" To them, *nothing* is impossible—and that's beautiful. As parents, our role is not to shrink their dreams to fit the world. It's to *expand the world* to match their dreams.

But visionary leadership isn't just about wild ideas—it's about *turning those dreams into direction*. It's taking what you imagine and working every day to make it real. As parents, it is natural to attempt to instill a sense of limitlessness in our children with the words, "You can be anything you want to be."

We our children then enthusiastically say, "Great! I want to be a giraffe!" we tend to reply, "no you cannot be a giraffe, but you can be anything else."

"OK well, when I grow up I want to be an Andean Condor!"

As parents, we often will slap our forehead and

say, "No you cannot be a condor, you are not a bird you are human. You can be anything you want to be that is realistic for humans."

Inadvertently, we discourage our children with these responses. We take their natural ability to dream and visualize with a dose of our understanding of the current version of reality. Perhaps Orville and Wilbur Wright witnessed the Andean Condor majestically in flight, the largest bird on the planet, and envisioned becoming just like that. Their persistence created the airplane.

Towering above all other land animals on earth at twenty feet tall, the giraffe is able to reach the highest branches in the Serengeti Plain in their African habitat. Perhaps this beautiful animal was the inspiration for building the Great Pyramid of Giza, the tallest man-made structure in the world for over 3,800 years.

Neither of these examples were "realistic" to achieve at the time of their creations. Someone had to look into their imagination to discover what could be, not just what is already there. Visionary leaders don't just focus on the present. Where others might see limits, Visionaries see potential. They look ahead. They ask big questions. Questions like *What kind of world do I want to help build?, How can my actions today shape someone's tomorrow? What legacy will I leave behind for others to follow?*

Visionaries don't wait for permission to act—they *lead with imagination, serve with action,* and *inspire through purpose.* The SPOILED Kid is the one who notices their school doesn't recycle and starts a student-led sustainability club. It's the teen who sees how her younger siblings struggle with reading and creates Storytime Saturdays to help them learn. It's the parent who turns a family recipe into a business—not just for income, but to teach their kids ownership and legacy.

Raising SPOILED kids means raising kids who can *see beyond themselves.* But to do that, parents must become visionary leaders in their own homes. You must believe in a future for your family that is greater than your past. You must talk about legacy, about impact, about how your child's name will be carried with honor long after you are gone.

Visionary parents ask:

- What kind of adults do I want my children to become?

- What do I want them to believe about themselves, their worth, and their place in the world?

- What values am I planting today that they'll pass on to their own children tomorrow?

We are not just raising kids. We are raising leaders. Business owners. Change agents. Bridge builders. Visionaries who will reshape communities, schools, and systems. But they can't do it if they don't first see it. And they can never see it if they are constantly being told to be realistic.

So we have to paint that picture for them. Speak life into them. Show them that every problem they notice is a chance to lead. Every gift they've been given is a tool for change. Every time they care, create, or dream—that's leadership in motion.

Teach your SPOILED Kids that they are never too young to dream boldly or to lead with heart. If they've ever had an idea that made people say, "That's never been done before,"—lean into it. Tell them that if they see something unfair, broken, or hurtful in your school or community, don't just say, "That's too bad." Ask, "*What can I do to change it?*" At the core of every great leader is vision. Not just the ability to see what is—but the courage to see what could be. Visionaries aren't afraid to dream bold dreams. They don't just follow maps; they draw new ones.

Keep in mind that Visionaries aren't always understood right away. Sometimes they're laughed at or told their ideas are too wild. But that never stops them. They hold onto hope, believe in possibility, and help others imagine a better future.

A SPOILED Kind visionary mind might look like the one who designs a robot that helps grandparents remember their medicine. Or who writes stories about heroes who fight injustice. Or who says, "One day, I'm going to start a company that gives every kid in the world clean water." These aren't just dreams. These are seeds of real leadership. As parents, we must protect those seeds—water them with belief, sunlight them with encouragement, and remove the weeds of doubt and fear. When we nurture vision, we raise leaders who create what the world needs next.

The great visionary Dr. Martin Luther King, Jr. once said, "You don't have to see the whole staircase to take the first step." Help your children believe that every step they take leads someone else closer to the top. Visionaries keep climbing and don't wait to lead—they *live like the future depends on them.* Because it does. Let's raise visionaries who lead with courage, who serve with purpose, and who dream so loudly that the world has no choice but to change. Because some of the world's most important movements, family legacies, innovations, inventions, and revolutions started with someone saying, "There has to be a better way."

Leadership 5.6:

Passive Inspiration - Leading by Being

In the world of visionary leadership, there is a quiet but powerful force that often goes unnoticed. It doesn't shout. It doesn't demand. It doesn't force others to follow. It simply *is*. We call this force *Passive Inspiration*. Passive Inspiration is the act of leading by living the values, discipline, and dreams you encourage in others. It is the deep understanding that true leadership is not about constant correction or loud direction. It's about consistent embodiment. It's about *being the lesson* before trying to *teach the lesson*.

When you walk into our café—or any of our family businesses—you'll immediately notice one thing: the words **PASSIVE INSPIRATION** displayed boldly above a mural of photographs. The mural tells a story: snapshots of our family ventures, milestones, struggles, and triumphs—each moment a testament to the journey we've dared to take together.

When we first began our company, we didn't set out to be "inspirational." We were simply pursuing a dream that had lived inside us for a long time. Yet almost immediately, we began receiving messages, calls, and conversations from people who said the same thing:

"I had this idea too, but I was too scared to move forward." "I didn't know how it would be received." "I wasn't sure if it was possible."

They had the dream, but what they were missing was the proof—the living, breathing example that it could be done. And it wasn't until we took the first step—risky, unsure, but determined—that those dreams inside others were reignited.

We turned *dreams into vision, vision into action, action into hustle, hustle into a business, and that business into a legacy.* And along the way, something beautiful happened: when others saw us doing it, they began to see themselves doing it too. We realized then the profound truth: By doing, we automatically become an inspiration. Especially to those who were silently waiting for someone to go first—even if they didn't consciously know they were waiting. That is the essence of Passive Inspiration. We didn't need a megaphone. We didn't need to shout. We just needed to move—boldly, quietly, consistently.

And it's the same with parenting. Every single day, we are leading our children, not only through the "big lessons" we intentionally try to teach but through the small, almost invisible actions we model:

- The way we speak about others when they're not around.

- The way we handle stress when plans don't go our way.
- The way we treat strangers, waiters, cashiers.
- The way we apologize when we're wrong.
- The way we dare to dream *and* the way we dare to fail.

Our children are watching. They are always watching—believe us! Often, what they catch from us is even more powerful than what we intentionally teach. Passive Inspiration reminds us that leadership is not a moment—it's a movement we embody with every choice we make. It's not about being perfect, but it is about being authentic. It's about walking the path we hope our children, and others, will someday have the courage to walk too.

When they are ready—when the *student* is ready—the *teacher* will appear. And sometimes, the teacher looks a lot like a parent who simply kept showing up, kept believing, kept trying, and kept loving—out loud, and on purpose.

Passive Inspiration is when you:

- **Read books at home** without forcing others to do the same—and your children pick up books because they see you doing it.
- **Apologize sincerely** when you make a mistake—and your children learn to do the same without a lecture.

- **Eat healthy, stay active, practice discipline**—and one day, a friend or a child asks, "How did you build that habit?"
- **Dream big and work quietly toward your goals**—and eventually someone you didn't even realize was watching says, "I want to do what you do."

Passive Inspiration is the ultimate form of *leading by example*. You do not push. You do not chase. You simply *are*. And when others are ready, they will come to you—not because you demanded, but because they recognize the quiet power you've been living out all along. We realized that not everyone is equipped to travel the journey with you. They may not see the vision as clearly as you. You don't have to argue people into greatness. You inspire them into greatness by becoming it yourself. And their vision gets a bit more clearer, the path so much less daunting or scary.

As parents, it's tempting to want immediate results. We want our kids to clean their rooms because we told them to. We want them to study because we said it's important. We want them to make good choices because we warned them. But you are raising SPOILED Kids, therefore, Passive Inspiration calls us to a deeper patience.

It says:

Be the kind of adult you want your child to become. Be the kind of leader you hope your child will one day be.

It means *consistently* modeling saving habits, entrepreneurial thinking, ownership mentality, discipline, and leadership—even when it seems like your children aren't paying attention. ANd they are most certainly always paying attention. Especially to your own inconsistencies to justify their own. When the moment is right, when they're ready to take their own step forward, they'll remember. They'll ask you, "How did you do it?" And because you've been living it all along, you'll be ready to guide them—not with empty words, but with real, lived wisdom.

Passive Inspiration requires strength: the strength to be consistent without needing applause, acknowledgment, or immediate validation. It trusts that seeds planted in silence will one day bear fruit. It understands that timing is not ours to control—but preparation is. Let your life speak much louder than your words. What you do will be the loudest, most sustaining sermon as a parent, you will ever preach.

Leadership isn't something your child will grow into "someday." It's something they can begin living today—in the way they treat people, solve problems, dream big, and make courageous choices.

Whether they are adapting to different personalities (Situational Leadership), serving their siblings with grace (Servant Leadership), sparking a new project or club (Transformational Leadership), or dreaming up the next big idea (Visionary Leadership)— your SPOILED kids are practicing leadership in real time. And so are you.

As a parent, you are not just raising a child—you are shaping a future. Before they ever meet a teacher, a coach, or a boss, **you** are their first and most influential leader. Every word you speak, every choice you make, every value you demonstrate becomes a living lesson. Your example is the curriculum they study daily. Your mindset becomes the mirror through which they learn to see themselves and the world around them.

When you lead with *purpose*, you teach them that life has meaning beyond the moment. When you lead with *presence*, you show them that love is spelled T-I-M-E—that attention and intentionality are more powerful than any lecture. And when you lead with *love*, you model the courage, empathy, and resilience they will one day need to lead themselves.

True leadership has never been about titles, authority, or control. It's not about being in charge— it's about being *in service*. It's about making things better: better choices for yourself, better opportunities for those around you, and a better world for the generations to come. Leadership is legacy work, and it begins right there in your home, in the ordinary moments that shape extraordinary futures.

So lead boldly—because your strength gives them courage. Lead humbly—because your humility teaches them humanity. And most importantly, lead now—because they are watching, learning, and absorbing more than you know. And even more importantly, they are ready—ready to rise, ready to reflect what they see in you, and ready to build on the foundation you lay.

PART 6:

ENTREPRENEURS

The sign was crooked, hand-painted in big, bold letters: **"Zenaya's Pet Sitting — Reliable and Fun!"** Next to it stood a young girl, clipboard in hand, ready to pitch her business to every neighbor walking by. She wasn't waiting for an allowance. She wasn't hoping someone would give her permission. This ambitious, beautifully-spirited, SPOILED kid saw a need, had an idea, and decided to *build* something by springing into action. She commercialized her compassion. That's entrepreneurship.

Coming home from an afternoon of playing basketball, our daughter, Zyla, offered to use the deep tissue massage gun and muscle cream to relieve the pain she saw her father experiencing. There was just one caveat: we first had to open her a point-of-sale account online so that she could receive the $5 payment she was asking for her services. Her rationale was that she did not like it when people were in pain and wanted to do something to help. Soon she was calling her grandparents, uncles, aunts, and to promote her business she named *Massage Yo Back Service*. This ambitious, beautifully-spirited, SPOILED kid saw a need, had an idea, and decided to *build* something by springing into action. She commercialized her compassion. That's entrepreneurship.

Zyon loves to express herself through baking. Nearly each day we can smell wonderful pastries cooking up in the oven or hear the mixer kneading dough that will eventually become some type of bread or cake or dessert. After learning how to make dough during a family activity she found her love of creating treats that warm the soul with their deliciousness. Friends and family alike are constantly raving about her culinary skills and often ask for her to make them something sweet and delicious. Understanding the value of her time and expense in materials to make her treats, she

Entrepreneurship is about more than starting a business or making a quick dollar. It's about seeing the world with curious eyes and a determined heart. It's asking: *What can I create? Who can I help? How can I build something bigger than me?* It's about ideas turned into action, and dreams fueled by courage.

Entrepreneurs have been changing the world since the beginning of time. Ancient traders sailed dangerous seas to bring new goods to new lands. Black entrepreneurs built thriving communities against impossible odds — from the brilliance of Black Wall Street to today's tech innovators and culture shapers. Every era of progress has been driven by people willing to bet on themselves—and their vision.

For a SPOILED Kid, it is not just about career choices; it's a way of seeing possibilities where others see limits. It's about:
- **Vision**: Dreaming of new solutions.
- **Grit**: Pushing through failure and setbacks.
- **Creativity**: Finding new ways to solve old problems.
  Service: Making life better for others while building for yourself.

And parents, your role is critical. You are the first "investor," the first "mentor," the first "partner." Whether it's a lemonade stand, a t-shirt brand, a YouTube channel, or a school club, every small venture plants seeds that grow into leadership, confidence, and ownership.

We have decided—with clarity and conviction—that we are not raising kids who simply exist to build someone else's dream. We are raising SPOILED Kids who will design, innovate, and lead; kids who are unafraid to take risks, unapologetic about their ambitions, and relentless in pursuit of their purpose.

Our children will be resilient in the face of failure, confident even when uncertainty surrounds them, and bold enough to create solutions when the world presents problems. They will understand the connection between earning, learning, and hard work—

knowing that success is not given, it is built.

We are not raising kids who must rely on others for their income, security, or impact. We are raising visionaries who will challenge limits, tear down barriers, and create their own opportunities. We are preparing them to build empires, not excuses.

Because entrepreneurship is not just about owning a business—it's about owning your life. It's about teaching our kids to shape their destiny, create pathways where none exist, and build a future filled with possibility.

In this journey, we're not just preparing them for the future. We're preparing them to shape it.

Entrepreneurs 6.1:

The Entrepreneurial Mindset

Entrepreneurship begins long before a business plan is written or a product is launched. It starts with a mindset—a way of seeing the world, making choices, and responding to challenges. In classrooms, careers, and everyday life, those who adopt an entrepreneurial mindset learn to look beyond what *is* and imagine what *could be*. They see opportunity where others see obstacles, and instead of waiting for permission, they create solutions, build value, and pursue meaningful change. Entrepreneurship isn't just about starting a business. It's about seeing the world differently—and choosing to create, rather than simply consume.

Beverly E. Jones writes extensively about developing clarity, resilience, and adaptability as a foundation for success. These qualities are central to the entrepreneurial mindset. To think like an entrepreneur, you must be willing to step into uncertainty, explore new paths, and experiment—even when you're unsure of the outcome. You must see failures not as defining moments but as stepping stones that lead you closer to innovation.

Richard Branson, founder of the Virgin Group, embodies this fearless curiosity. His approach shows us that entrepreneurship isn't about having all the answers from the start; it's about being bold enough to try, creative enough to adapt, and relentless enough to continue when others quit. His career reflects one of the most important principles of this mindset: risk isn't something to be feared; it's something to be managed, learned from, and leveraged.

Entrepreneurship Beyond Business

One of the most important insights from Gary G. Schoeniger's work, particularly in *Entrepreneurship: The Practice and Mindset (3rd Edition)*, is that entrepreneurship isn't confined to running a company. It's a practice—a way of thinking and problem-solving that applies to every area of life.

In schools, it looks like the student who sees a better way to organize a group project and takes initiative to lead. In careers, it's the employee who identifies inefficiencies in the workplace and proposes improvements instead of waiting for someone else to act. In families, it's parents modeling resourcefulness, teaching children how to create opportunities instead of depending on others to provide them.

In this sense, the entrepreneurial mindset is deeply connected to choice. Every day we choose how to respond to challenges, setbacks, and opportunities. M. Lalia Helmer reminds us that great innovators combine empathy with strategy; they observe human needs deeply and build solutions that serve people better. That is just as relevant in relationships, education, and personal growth as it is in business. When children learn this early, they stop looking for "the right answer" and start creating their own.

Our Journey to the Mindset

Our personal path to adopting the entrepreneurial mindset—both for ourselves and for our family—has been a lifetime in the making. It didn't happen overnight, nor did it come without challenges. It's been shaped by seasons of sacrifice, years of growth, and lessons learned through trial and error. While classrooms and books have taught us many things, there are some lessons only lived experience can provide. The mistakes, the pivots, the unexpected turns—each became a stepping stone, shaping not just what we do, but how we think.

But here's the truth: we didn't build this mindset alone. Like you, we've done what you're doing right now—learning from others, reading their ideas, studying their strategies, and allowing their wisdom to refine our own thinking. We've drawn inspiration from those who came before us, who dared to dream big, face obstacles, and still carve paths where none existed. Their voices continue to push us, challenge us, and ignite new possibilities in our minds.

Some of our favorite authors, educators, and visionaries have taught us profound lessons about the entrepreneurial mindset—not just as a tool for business, but as a framework for living, leading, and thriving. Dave Ramsey showed us the power of financial freedom and intentional stewardship. Richard Branson showed us how courage and creativity can turn limitations into opportunities. Gary Schoeniger's insights on problem-solving and ownership reshaped how we approach challenges in every area of life. Pinkett and Robinson, in *Black Faces in High Places*, gave us both representation and strategy—teaching us what it looks like to succeed and lead boldly while staying rooted in purpose. Beverly E. Jones and M. Lalia Helmer reminded us that empathy and adaptability are as important as innovation when shaping a sustainable future.

We absorbed their teachings, internalized their strategies, and—most importantly—we modeled them for our children. Because raising SPOILED Kids isn't just about talking to them about leadership, creativity, and ownership. It's about showing them what these values look like in action. We've invited them into our wins and our struggles, into the late-night brainstorming sessions and big "aha" moments, letting them see firsthand that entrepreneurship is not a single act—it's a way of thinking, living, and creating.

This journey is ongoing. We are still students of this mindset, still evolving, still learning, and still becoming. But what we know for certain is this: the entrepreneurial mindset is contagious. When parents embody it, children absorb it. And when families cultivate it together, they unlock a generational power that builds not just businesses, but legacies.

Representation, Purpose, and Legacy

For Black families and communities, entrepreneurship carries an even deeper weight. In *Black Faces in High Places*, Randal Pinkett and Jeffery Robinson explore how Black entrepreneurs and executives navigate spaces where opportunity has historically been limited. Their work highlights an essential truth: entrepreneurship is not only about building wealth; it's about claiming ownership of your future, rewriting narratives, and breaking systemic barriers.

Representation matters. When children see entrepreneurs who look like them, they gain permission to dream bigger, to imagine themselves as innovators, and to lead boldly. But representation alone isn't enough—we must also equip the next generation with tools, strategies, and mindsets that empower them to build pathways where none exist. By combining personal ambition with collective responsibility, today's entrepreneurs create businesses that strengthen families, uplift communities, and redefine possibilities.

The Entrepreneurial Mindset Framework

The entrepreneurial mindset can be practiced, modeled, and mastered. This five-step framework helps parents and kids activate their inner entrepreneur:

1. **See Differently**: Train your mind to notice opportunities where others see problems.
2. **Think Creatively**: Use imagination, design thinking, and innovation to craft bold solutions.
3. **Act Boldly**: Take smart risks, experiment, and learn from failure rather than fearing it.
4. **Build with Purpose**: Root your work in values, empathy, and service to others.
5. **Own Your Future**: Make disciplined decisions about money, time, and resources that create freedom and choice.

When we teach our children to live this way, we don't just prepare them for success—we prepare them to create success.

ENTREPRENEURS 6.2:

The Ideal Idea

Have you ever been somewhere, seen something, and thought to yourself—or even said out loud—*"You know, they should..."* followed by an idea that would make life simpler, better, or more efficient? We've all had those moments—flashes of creativity when we see a solution that no one else seems to have acted on yet. That's where innovation begins. That's where entrepreneurs are born.

We had one of those moments while visiting Puerto Rico. The sun was warm, the music was lively, and the air was full of delicious smells from a park filled with food trucks, each one decorated beautifully and buzzing with hungry customers. Our stomachs growled in anticipation as we wandered from truck to truck, expecting to find a little piece of vegan heaven tucked into the vibrant food scene.

But after scanning menu after menu, our excitement turned into frustration—not a single truck had vegan options. We settled for a couple of snacks, but we left unsatisfied, disappointed, and honestly, a little annoyed.

Then it happened. We looked at each other

and said, *"You know, there really should be an all-vegan food truck—especially back home."* But here's where the story shifts. Instead of leaving that thought floating in the air, waiting for someone else to solve the problem, we made a decision: *"We are they."*

We stopped waiting for "they" to do it. We stopped believing that innovation belonged to someone else. That moment of frustration became the spark of an idea—the seed that would eventually grow into Black Leaf Vegan.

And that's the essence of entrepreneurship: seeing a gap, imagining what could be, and stepping up to create the solution yourself. It's about taking ownership of your ideas, your vision, and your future—not hoping that someone else will bring them to life.

When it comes to entrepreneurship, one truth stands strong: every thriving business, every groundbreaking innovation, every life-changing movement began the same way—with an idea. But here's the secret most people overlook: great ideas don't usually fall from the sky. They aren't lightning bolts striking out of nowhere. They are discovered through curiosity, shaped through persistence, and refined through creativity and collaboration. Ideas grow out of questions, out of frustrations, out of the quiet whispers of *"what if?"* and the bold declarations of *"why not me?"*.

Every empire we admire today—from world-changing companies to cultural movements that reshaped society—started small. They started as half-formed thoughts scribbled on napkins, conversations whispered late at night, or frustrations turned into fuel for innovation.

An idea by itself is just potential. It becomes powerful when someone decides to act on it, nurture it, and invite others to join in building it. That's the heart of entrepreneurship: taking what begins as a spark and fanning it into a flame that lights the way for others

For SPOILED Kids, developing the right idea is less about waiting for inspiration and more about creating a space for innovation to happen. That means exploring possibilities, asking the right questions, and sometimes failing forward—because even the "wrong" idea can lead to the *right* one.

Ideas are the seeds of entrepreneurship. They are the sparks that ignite movements, the blueprints behind solutions, and the foundation on which businesses are built. Without ideas, there is no innovation, and without innovation, there is no growth.

For kids and parents alike, understanding this is critical: the most successful entrepreneurs are not the ones who have the first idea, but the ones who develop the best idea by thinking differently and staying persistent.

Your "ideal idea" may come from:
- Seeing a problem and deciding to solve it.

- Spotting a trend before others notice it.
- Creating something fun, useful, or unique that people want.
- Combining two unrelated ideas to make something completely new.

To find "the ideal idea," we have to create environments where imagination thrives. Brainstorming isn't just tossing thoughts around randomly; it's a structured process of generating possibilities without fear of judgment.

Here are a few brainstorming strategies to try as a family:

1. Mind Mapping

Start with one big word or concept in the middle of a page—like "business," "fun," or "helping people." Branch out with connected ideas, then connect *those* ideas to others. This creates a visual web that unlocks creativity.

2. The "What If" Game

Ask wild, open-ended questions:
- *What if* we could make homework fun? *What if* pets could talk?
- *What if* we could turn trash into art?
- No idea is too silly—sometimes the "crazy" ones spark genius solutions.

3. Role-Storming

Pretend to be someone else—a famous inventor, a CEO, a chef, an athlete—and ask, "How would *they* solve this problem?" Kids love stepping into creative roles, and it unlocks unexpected perspectives.

4. Reverse Thinking

Instead of asking, "How do we solve this problem?" ask, "How would we make it *worse*?" Then flip those "bad ideas" into potential solutions.

In entrepreneurship, one of the most powerful tools for developing ideas is the Ideate stage of Design Thinking. Design Thinking is a method innovators use to create human-centered solutions, and the *Ideate stage* focuses on generating as many creative possibilities as possible without judgment.

Here's how to guide kids through the Ideate stage:

1. **Understand the Problem**: Clarify what you're trying to solve.

2. **Go Wide with Ideas**: No idea is too small or too silly at this stage.

3. **Encourage Wild Thinking**: Sometimes the "impossible" ideas are the ones that lead to breakthroughs.

4. **Build on Each Other's Ideas**: Listen, collaborate, and combine thoughts.

5. **Narrow and Select**: After exploration, choose the best ideas to test first.

This process teaches your SPOILED Kids to think big, stay flexible, and innovate without fear of failure.

An "ideal idea" often comes from breaking rules and challenging limits. Entrepreneurs thrive when they look at what exists and ask, *"How can I make this better?"* or *"What hasn't been done yet?"*

Encourage your kids to: **Look for problems others ignore.** Every inconvenience is a potential opportunity. **Experiment fearlessly.** Not every idea works, but every attempt teaches something. **Stay curious.** Ask "why" and "what if" more often. The most powerful businesses—from tech giants to neighborhood start-ups—came from ordinary people who dared to reimagine the world around them.

Once you've brainstormed and selected an idea, the next step is turning it into action: Test it. Refine it. Try it again. Improve it until it works. Teaching kids this cycle helps them understand that failure is feedback, and that innovation isn't a straight line—it's an evolving journey. For our SPOILED Kids—and their parents—the goal isn't to have the *perfect* idea right away. The goal is to stay curious, stay creative, and stay courageous. Your ideal idea will grow as you grow. It will start small, take shape, and become something greater than you imagined.

Because the future belongs to those who dare to imagine it first.

ENTREPRENEURS 6.3:

Entrepreneurs are Leaders

Entrepreneurship and leadership are often discussed separately, but in reality, they are deeply connected. We separate them in the book only to distinguish that all Entrepreneurs are Leaders, but not all Leaders have an entrepreneurial mind. An entrepreneur creates opportunities by envisioning what doesn't yet exist; a leader mobilizes people to bring that vision to life. You can have a groundbreaking idea, but without the ability to inspire, guide, and influence others, your idea will rarely grow beyond your imagination.

Richard Branson, one of the most daring entrepreneurs of our time, once said, *"Business opportunities are like buses; there's always another one coming."* But his career shows us something more important—vision without leadership has limits. Branson built the Virgin brand into a global powerhouse because he knew how to build teams, inspire innovation, and cultivate trust. In other words, entrepreneurship sparks the fire, but leadership sustains the flame.

An entrepreneur isn't just responsible for creating solutions; they must guide others through uncertainty, motivate action, and inspire collaboration.

A business idea, no matter how brilliant, needs people to execute it, refine it, and scale it. This is where leadership becomes critical.

Leadership in entrepreneurship involves:
- **Defining the Vision**: Painting a clear picture of where the venture is headed and why it matters.
- **Building Trust**: Creating environments where people feel valued, included, and motivated.
- **Making Decisions Under Pressure**: Choosing courage even when the outcome is uncertain.
- **Inspiring Action**: Encouraging others to join the mission and contribute their strengths.

This doesn't just apply to business. Leadership shapes how entrepreneurs influence schools, communities, and entire industries. A SPOILED Kid who learns to think like both an entrepreneur and a leader doesn't just start ventures—they rally others to build lasting impact together.

To understand the power of leadership within entrepreneurship, we can look at the story of Indra Nooyi, the former CEO of PepsiCo and one of the most influential Indian-American business leaders of all time. Born in Chennai, India, Indra built her career by challenging expectations, embracing bold ideas, and inspiring those around her to dream bigger.

When she became CEO, she didn't just manage PepsiCo; she reimagined it. She led with an entrepreneurial spirit, introducing innovative product strategies and championing healthier alternatives—anticipating consumer needs before the market demanded them. But more importantly, she modeled inclusive leadership, creating pathways for other women and minorities to rise into positions of influence.

Indra's journey shows our children something powerful: representation matters, but so does innovation. Leadership isn't about maintaining the status quo; it's about changing the game and bringing others with you.

Entrepreneurial leaders thrive by:

- Thinking beyond limitations and imagining bold possibilities.
- Listening deeply to the needs of people and markets.
  Building diverse teams that bring new perspectives to the table.
- Demonstrating empathy, discipline, and adaptability—qualities that inspire others to follow.

When we raise our kids to embody these traits, they learn that leadership isn't about power—it's about purpose and people. They begin to see themselves not just as problem-solvers but as builders of communities, movements, and legacies.

Teaching kids the connection between leadership and entrepreneurship begins with modeling it at home. When children see you solving problems creatively, managing challenges thoughtfully, and taking ownership of your vision, they learn firsthand what it means to lead by example.

Encourage your kids to take on leadership roles early:
- When they dream up a business idea, challenge them to organize a team and delegate responsibilities.
- When they join group projects in school, teach them to step forward, set goals, and guide collaboration.
- When they face setbacks, remind them that leadership begins with leading yourself first—staying focused, resilient, and ready to try again.

The entrepreneurial leader isn't defined by what they start. They're defined by how they empower others to grow alongside them.

The SPOILED Philosophy in Action

Within the SPOILED leadership and entrepreneurship naturally work hand in hand because Entrepreneurs imagine opportunities. They are Leaders who mobilize people and resources to bring them to life. They are Disciplined dreamers who sustain the vision for long-term impact.

By teaching kids to embody both roles, we prepare them not just to create businesses, but to build legacies. When our children understand that they have the power to innovate and the ability to inspire others, they step confidently into the role of change-makers.

Entrepreneurs see possibilities, but leaders make them real. One cannot truly thrive without the other. A great idea without leadership rarely leaves the notebook. A passionate leader without vision rarely inspires lasting change. But when the two come together—when vision aligns with influence—innovation expands, communities strengthen, and the impossible becomes achievable.

For SPOILED Kids, understanding this relationship early unlocks the ability to not just dream, but to mobilize others to dream with them. It reminds them that entrepreneurship is not a solo journey. It's a collective mission.

Because leadership doesn't just elevate your ideas. It amplifies your impact.

Entrepreneurs 6.4:

Fear vs Failure

People often say, *"Failure is not an option."* But the truth is, failure is not only an option—it is inevitable. If you are truly stretching yourself, if you are building, testing, experimenting, and daring, you will stumble. You will fall. You will miscalculate. You will fail. And that's okay. Failure is not the end of the journey; it is part of the map.

The real enemy isn't failure—it's fear. Fear is the invisible chain that holds dreams hostage. Fear is what keeps you staring at your vision board instead of taking steps toward it. Fear whispers lies in your ear: *"You're not ready. You're not qualified. You're not enough."* Fear is the one that convinces you to shrink when you were born to expand.

Left unchecked, fear will string you along with no GPS, sending you in circles. It will trap you in the rat race, chasing goals that were never truly yours, with no real intention of breaking free. Fear leaves you yearning for freedom but never taking the leap to claim it.

Failure, on the other hand, is simply an event, not an identity. It is not permanent, and it is never fatal. Failure is a teacher, sometimes tough but always truthful. Every failed attempt brings with it feedback: what works, what doesn't, and what might work better next time. Some of history's greatest entrepreneurs, inventors, and leaders—from Thomas Edison to Oprah Winfrey, from Richard Branson to countless local visionaries—failed more times than most people even tried. Their resilience wasn't in avoiding failure, but in refusing to let failure define them.

That's why in entrepreneurship the mantra is not *"avoid failure"* but *"JUMP!"* Leap. Move forward. Try, test, refine, and course-correct as you go. The entrepreneurial mindset thrives not because it avoids mistakes, but because it refuses to be paralyzed by fear. As the saying goes, *"If you haven't failed, you haven't tried."*

Fear silences creativity. It stalls progress. It traps you in endless cycles of hesitation. It magnifies the consequences of failure until they feel unbearable. But fear is a liar. The greater risk is not failing—it's never starting. It's never risking. It's never becoming who you were designed to be.

The difference between those who succeed and those who stay stuck is rarely talent, intelligence, or luck. It's the courage to act despite uncertainty. Entrepreneurs understand that progress often feels like jumping out of an airplane and building the parachute on the way down. You may not land exactly where you intended, but you will learn how to adjust, how to innovate, and how to trust your preparation, your intuition, and your network to guide you safely. So let's be clear: failure is not the enemy. Fear is.

And this is the lesson we must give our children. To raise SPOILED Kids with an entrepreneurial mindset, we must teach them not to fear falling down but to fear standing still. Not to fear making mistakes but to fear making none—because that would mean they never tried. The road to entrepreneurship is not paved with perfection but with experiments, resilience, and the wisdom that comes from each attempt.

Failure is part of the process. Fear should never be part of the plan.

To manage this fear effectively:
1. **Adopt a Growth Mindset:** View failures as learning opportunities rather than setbacks. This will mean that you can not stay in the negative (I knew this would happen) stage long. Embracing this perspective allows you to learn from mistakes and continuously improve. While wallowing in the issue will have you quitting, digging in to do the hard work or avoiding opportunities.
2. **Set Realistic Goals:** Break down larger objectives into manageable tasks. Achieving these smaller milestones can build confidence and reduce the intimidation factor of larger

goals. Overloading yourself does not make you more productive. Most times it can make you procrastinate and fall short of the initial task.

3. **Seek Mentorship and Support:** Engage with experienced entrepreneurs or join business networks. Using mentors, or other business professionals insights and experiences can provide guidance and reassurance, helping you navigate challenges more effectively. It will allow you to have a safe space to voice concerns and challenges in a safe space.

4. **Embrace Calculated Risks:** Recognize that risk-taking is integral to entrepreneurship. By carefully assessing and managing risks, you can make informed decisions that drive growth and innovation.

5. **Practice Resilience:** Develop the ability to bounce back from setbacks. Viewing challenges as opportunities to improve can strengthen your resolve and adaptability.

6. **Utilize Rejection Therapy:** Consider engaging in activities that expose you to rejection in controlled settings. This practice can desensitize you to the fear of failure and build confidence.

By implementing these strategies, you can transform the fear of failure into a motivating force, propelling your entrepreneurial journey forward.

ENTREPRENEURS 6.5:

The Power of a Simple Stand

Imagine your child standing proudly in front of a lemonade stand on a warm summer day. Their smile stretches wide, not only because they sold a cup of lemonade, but because they created something of their own. With nothing more than an idea, some supplies, and determination, they took a risk, worked hard, and made it happen.

That's entrepreneurship. And it's one of the most powerful gifts we can give our kids.

Entrepreneurship is far more than starting a business. It is a way of seeing the world differently. It's the mindset that notices a problem and thinks, *I can fix that*. It's the courage to spot an opportunity and say, *Why not me?* It is the heartbeat of creativity, leadership, ownership, and resilience all working together. At its core, it is the belief that we are not here simply to take part—we are here to build, shape, and lead.

This spirit of entrepreneurship is not new. Long before the age of tech startups and social-media millionaires, entrepreneurship thrived in every corner of the world. Ancient traders crossed deserts and oceans with caravans of spices, silk, and precious goods. Inventors in every era transformed wild dreams into practical realities that reshaped how people lived and worked.

And closer to home, our own history is full of entrepreneurs who built not only businesses, but communities. Black entrepreneurs, in particular, carved out thriving centers of commerce and culture, from the brilliance of Black Wall Street in Tulsa to the salons, restaurants, shops, and startups of today. Even in the face of closed doors and systemic obstacles, they proved that vision and persistence could not be denied.

The SPOILED Kid Perspective

For a SPOILED Kid entrepreneurship isn't just a career option to consider someday. It's a mindset for life. It's learning to ask: *What can I create? How can I help? What problems can I solve? How do I bounce back when things get tough?* These questions are the foundation of resilience, creativity, and growth. They teach children to look at the world as builders, not just as consumers.

The Parent's Role

But here's the truth: this journey begins with us, the parents. It is not enough to tell our children they can succeed; we must show them. We show them what it looks like to dream boldly, to hustle smart, and to build with heart. We model entrepreneurship when we turn kitchen-table talks into brainstorming sessions, when we turn small chores into leadership opportunities, and when we turn setbacks into lessons rather than excuses.

Our children are watching not just what we say, but how we move. They learn courage by seeing us take risks. They learn creativity by watching us solve problems. They learn resilience by witnessing us rise after setbacks.

Entrepreneurs 6.6:

The Black Leaf Vegan Story

It started with a simple but powerful frustration: there weren't enough healthy, plant-based dining options in our community. Everywhere we went, we saw the same thing—fast food chains, limited vegan choices, and very few spaces that truly celebrated **culture, health, and community** all in one.

Time after time, we'd find ourselves surrounded by options but with nothing that truly aligned with our values and lifestyle. We'd search for something plant-based, flavorful, and fulfilling—something that nourished the body and honored the culture—but too often, we walked away disappointed.

And that's when the moment came: *"You know, there really should be an all-vegan food truck... especially back home."*

But instead of waiting for "they" to do it, we realized we were "they" we were speaking of. And realizing this, the vision was born—to create something different, something intentional, and something that served not just food, but purpose. That Vision became a Dream. Our dream became a hustle. Our hustle became a business. And our business is creating a legacy.

The Hustle: Turning Dreams Into Action

A dream without action remains a wish. We started small but moved boldly. Nights at the kitchen table turned into early mornings sourcing ingredients, experimenting with recipes, and learning the business side of food entrepreneurship from the ground up.

There were long lines because we had not yet perfected the preparation process, generator failures, unpredictable weather, and plenty of moments when quitting would have been easier. But the dream was bigger than the discomfort. With first a borrowed grill from our brother-in-law, a tent and our recipes we began this journey. We eventually were able to purchase a trailer that we gutted and created our first truck. With an unmatched enthusiasm we engaged with every single customer, and poured everything we had into building something special.

We weren't just selling food. We were creating an experience. We were inviting people to taste something different—to imagine that healthy food could be flavorful, beautiful, and connected to culture.

The Breakthrough: From Truck to Brand

Word spread fast. People lined up, brought friends, and told their families. And just like that, Black Leaf Vegan evolved from a single food truck into a registered trademarked growing lifestyle brand.

We expanded into multiple trucks and locations,

introduced new menu items and began hosting events at our flagship cafe that fused food, fitness, culture, and community securing hundreds of thousands of dollars in grant monies from the State, County and professional sports teams in our home city. Black Leaf Vegan became more than a place to eat—it became a hub for empowerment, ownership, inspiration, and connection, opening doors we never imagined possible. We were invited to speak internationally, sharing our story of entrepreneurship, plant-based living, global citizenry, and community empowerment. We traveled across the globe, connecting with changemakers and culture-shapers, carrying the message that ownership and vision have no borders.

Our family became a part of the journey, learning as we built. Through our travels, our children gained exposure to new cultures, new foods, and new perspectives. Every flight, every event, every conversation became part of their education—showing them firsthand what it looks like to build something bigger than yourself. We grew beyond the delicious plant-based food that we served to become a movement.

We launched a clothing line inspired by plant-based living and empowerment. We developed partnerships with schools, businesses, and organizations to promote wellness and entrepreneurship. And through our work with the SPOILED Kids framework we began planting seeds of generational wealth by teaching families how to build ownership together.

Therefore, Black Leaf Vegan is no longer just a business. Because of our Entrepreneurial Mindset and ability to work collaboratively to execute our dreams, it is now a blueprint for what happens when vision meets courage, and hustle meets heart.

We started with one dream. That dream became a food truck. That food truck became a brand. That brand became a platform. And now, that platform is building a legacy—one rooted in:

- **Ownership**: creating spaces we control and businesses we grow.
- **Family**: working, building, and traveling together.
- **Community**: giving back, creating opportunities, and inspiring change.
- **Impact**: showing others that their dreams are valid, possible, and achievable.

The journey is ongoing, but one thing is certain: we are not done yet. Black Leaf Vegan isn't just about food. It's about freedom, culture, and the power of vision.

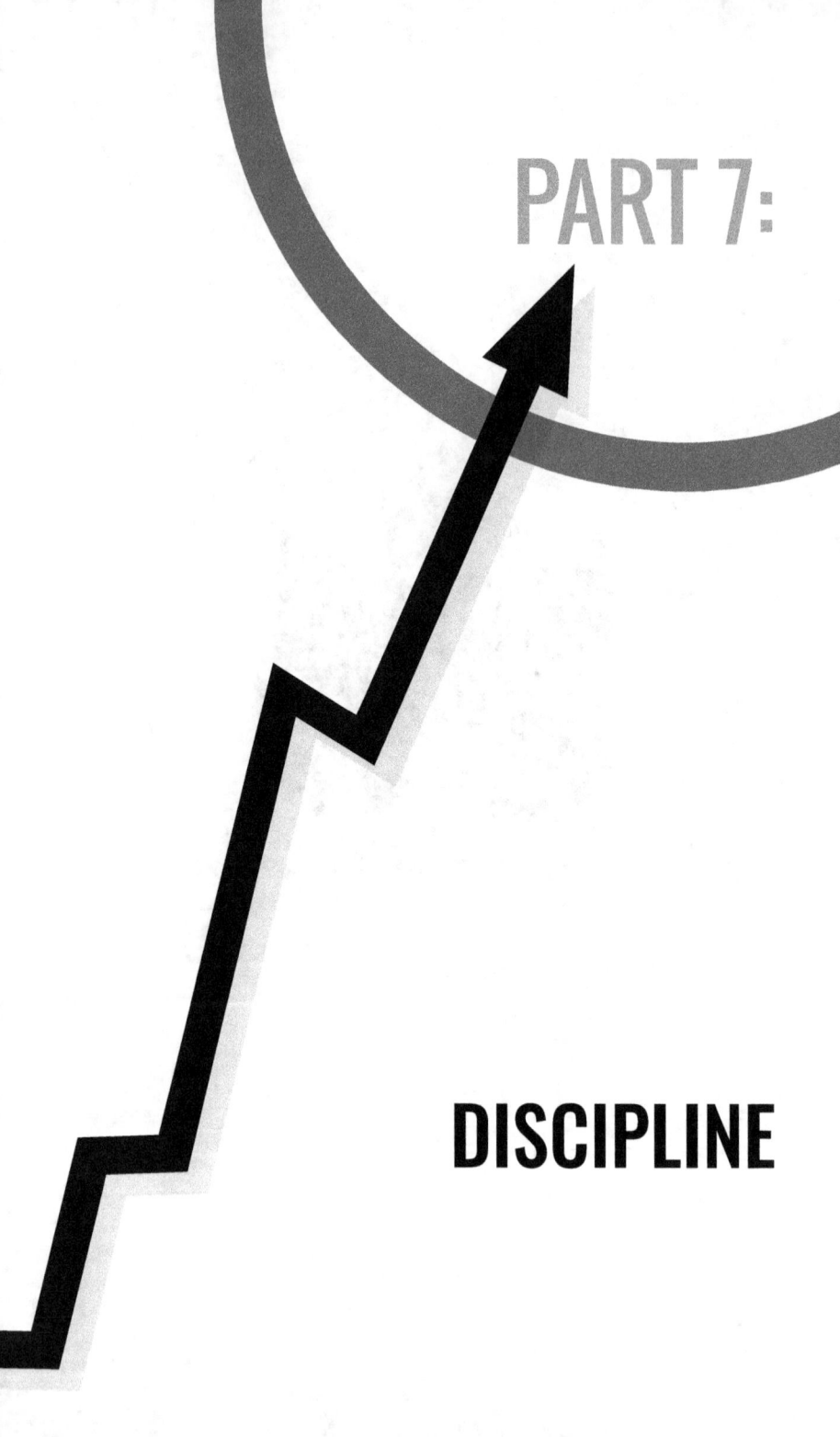

PART 7:

DISCIPLINE

" Here's to the crazy ones. The misfits. The rebels. The troublemakers. The round pegs in the square holes... Because the people who are crazy enough to think they can change the world, are the ones who do." – Steve Jobs. These words are often celebrated as a rallying cry for boldness, vision, and unconventional thinking, yet behind every daring idea, every act of courage, every spark that challenges the status quo, there lies a quieter force that rarely gets the same attention: discipline.

Passion, creativity, and bravery can ignite movements, but without discipline they burn out quickly, leaving only smoke. With discipline, however, that spark is not wasted; it is fanned into a steady flame that can light the way forward, generation after generation. Discipline is not merely one of the qualities of a SPOILED Kid—it is the foundation upon which all the others rest. To be a Saver, Producer, Owner, Investor, Leader, and Entrepreneur requires imagination and courage, but to bring those qualities together into something lasting demands the discipline to stay focused, consistent, and resilient when distractions lure, when doubts whisper, and when difficulties press in. Discipline is the thread that weaves the SPOILED framework into a fabric strong enough to endure the weight of life.

The very word discipline carries with it centuries of wisdom, derived from the Latin disciplina, meaning instruction, training, and knowledge. It was never meant to be equated with punishment or restriction but with the intentional shaping of a mind, body, and spirit toward excellence. At its essence, discipline is not about confinement but about freedom. A SPOILED Kid who embraces discipline does not see it as a cage but as wings. Discipline frees them from being controlled by impulse, fatigue, or fear. It builds within them an inner scaffolding that allows them to climb higher and stay balanced when the winds of life blow strong. It is the long game—patience in the face of frustration, structure in the face of chaos, determination in the face of doubt. It transforms fragile dreams into durable realities.

A disciplined SPOILED Kid is more than a dreamer; they are a doer. They are hungry for knowledge but never satisfied with learning alone; they insist on applying what they learn, even when results come slowly. They show up when others quit. They practice when others rest. They stay the course when shortcuts seem tempting. They understand that discipline is the bridge between intention and impact, between desire and destiny.

And when storms come, as they surely do, they endure them not as victims but as visionaries. They have the grit to remain rooted while winds rage and the wisdom to see setbacks as stepping stones rather than stumbling blocks. They know that consistency compounds—every habit repeated, every principle practiced, every effort sustained eventually grows into wealth, stability, and legacy.

Discipline also teaches balance, because life is not linear and progress is rarely neat. A disciplined child pursues goals with relentless focus, yet remains adaptable when circumstances shift. They bend without breaking, adjust without abandoning, and carry optimism rooted not in wishful thinking but in action. Their confidence is not arrogance but assurance—assurance that they have laid a foundation strong enough to bear the weight of their own dreams and steady enough to hold up the dreams of those who come after them.

At its highest form, discipline is not cold, rigid, or joyless. True discipline is guided by kindness, fueled by purpose, and anchored in love. It teaches children to use their focus and determination not merely to advance themselves, but to strengthen relationships, nurture communities, and plant seeds that will yield fruit for others. In this way, discipline expands from a personal practice into a legacy—not just a way of surviving life, but a way of shaping it, influencing it, and leaving it better than it was found.

DISCIPLINE 7.1:

The 4 Corners of Discipline

When most people hear the word *discipline*, they think of strict rules, punishment, or rigid routines. But true discipline isn't about restriction—it's about liberation. For us, discipline is the foundation of freedom. It's the steady foundation that allows dreams to grow tall without toppling over. Discipline is what transforms vision into reality, potential into performance, and good intentions into lasting legacies.

In our family, discipline has never been about perfection. It has always been about persistence. We tell our daughters all the time: "You don't have to get it right every time—but you do have to show up, try again, and stay committed." That is the essence of discipline. It is the glue that holds every other piece of being a SPOILED Kid together and thriving.

Through our experiences, education, readings, and observations of people we greatly admire, we have identified the four essential practices of discipline. Think of them like the four corners of a sturdy house whose foundation is set deep into the ground. Without them, the house collapses. With them, you can build a home that stands for generations.

1. **Delaying Gratification**

    We have already introduced the concept of Delayed Gratification in previous chapters, but it is so important to helping raise the complete SPOILED Kid, that it is worth revisiting. Discipline, like Saving, Producing, Investing, and other concepts we have provided, begins with the ability to delay gratification—to choose long-term reward over short-term pleasure. This is one of the hardest lessons to teach children in a world that says, "Have it now."

    We can remember when Zenaya wanted a new pair of shoes. She had the money from chores and small business sales, but she also had a goal: saving for her trip abroad. We sat down together and weighed the options. Did she want the instant excitement of new shoes, or the life-changing experience of walking streets in another country? With some nudging, she chose to wait. Weeks later, when she was exploring Cartagena with us, she understood the power of waiting. That lesson will outlast any shoe. Delaying gratification is the muscle that builds resilience. It's the difference between eating the marshmallow now or saving it for something sweeter later.

2. **Taking Responsibility**

Discipline requires ownership. To be disciplined means to stop blaming circumstances, stop blaming other people, and take responsibility for your actions and outcomes.

When we started the food truck for Black Leaf Vegan, nothing went as planned in those early days. Generators failed, lines grew too long, customers complained. We could have blamed the city, the weather, or even the customers. Instead, we chose responsibility: fix the generator, refine our system, improve communication. That's discipline. And it's the same lesson we want our daughters to learn—when things fall apart, don't point fingers. Pick up the tools and rebuild. Responsibility isn't about guilt; it's about power. When you own the problem, you also own the solution.

3. Commitment to Truth

Discipline is also about honesty—with yourself, with others, and with reality. It's easy to lie to ourselves, to pretend everything is fine when it's not, or to take shortcuts instead of confronting the truth. But discipline demands we face reality head-on.

Our family has learned this through financial transparency. When we bought our first rental property at the tax sale for $750, the temptation was to get excited and jump in without running all the numbers. But discipline meant sitting down with spreadsheets, calculating renovation costs, and admitting the hard truths: this would take time, money, and sweat. No illusions. Just honesty.

Our girls watched us do the math, argue a little, pray, and then commit. That honesty gave them a model:

discipline means you don't hide from the truth—you embrace it, because only then can you build something real.

4. Balancing

Finally, discipline is about balance. Life pulls us in every direction—family, business, travel, school, community. Without discipline, we tilt too far one way and everything suffers. Balance doesn't mean equal time for everything; it means the right time for the right thing.

On our Road School journey, there will be days when the girls just want to play and explore, and days when we must pause and do math, write journals, or read books. Discipline is the balance that makes room for both joy and duty, fun and focus. It teaches them that yes, you can have adventure—but you must also stay grounded.

Balance is what makes a disciplined life sustainable. It's not all grind and no rest, nor all play and no progress. It's learning the art of weaving the two.

Discipline 7.2:

The Quiet Genius

To raise a disciplined SPOILED Kid is to give them more than the tools of personal success; it is to equip them with the strength to expand a family's legacy. Discipline is the hinge on which everything else swings. Without it, money may be earned, but quickly lost; businesses may be launched, but collapse under the weight of inconsistency; and leadership may be claimed, but crumble without integrity. Discipline ensures that wealth is not just accumulated but preserved, that opportunities are not just seized but maximized, and that influence is not just exercised but stewarded with care.

A disciplined child is not merely successful—they are a multiplier. Their consistency magnifies their creativity. Their patience deepens their leadership. Their focus sharpens their entrepreneurship. Their steadiness transforms fleeting gains into lasting prosperity. The wealth they create is not limited to financial capital but extends into the relational bonds they nurture, the spiritual roots they develop, and the cultural legacies they build. With discipline, what they generate will outlast them, blessing children, grandchildren, and entire communities.

Raising a disciplined SPOILED Kid is never about perfection; perfection is a mirage that distracts and disappoints. Discipline is about cultivating persistence, purpose, and principle. It is about teaching children to stand up after they fall, to keep walking when the path is steep, and to stay steady when distractions shout for attention. A disciplined child learns that shortcuts rarely lead to long-term success, that excuses weaken the will, and that responsibility—though heavy at times—makes them strong enough to carry their dreams.

These children grow into adults who do more than win for themselves. They enrich every space they enter. They uplift teammates, families, organizations, and neighborhoods because discipline gives them the ability to endure what others avoid, to finish what others abandon, and to model what others only preach. When the world grows complicated, when pressures mount, and when temptations whisper, they will not scatter or fold. They will respond with resilience, act with wisdom, and lead with love.

Discipline is often overlooked because it lacks glamour. It is quiet, steady, and unflashy. Yet it is this very quietness that makes it powerful. Discipline is the silent architect behind every achievement, the invisible rhythm that keeps progress moving forward. It is the structure that allows bold ideas to thrive, the endurance that keeps visions alive, and the strength that turns today's small steps into tomorrow's legacy. Without discipline, brilliance fizzles; with discipline, brilliance compounds.

When you raise a disciplined child, you are not simply shaping their future—you are gifting the world a leader, a builder, and a legacy maker. You are planting a tree whose roots will hold firm in storms, whose branches will stretch to shelter others, and whose fruit will feed generations yet to come. Discipline is not just the practice of rules; it is the practice of freedom. It liberates children from impulsive living, shields them from destructive patterns, and empowers them to create with intention. It is the unseen genius that makes greatness possible.

DISCIPLINE 7.3:

You are What You Do Most

Discipline is often misunderstood as a matter of sheer willpower, as if success belongs only to the strongest, the most stubborn, or the rare few who can grit their teeth longer than everyone else. But the truth is far more hopeful: discipline is not about force; it is about design. It is less about pushing through with brute strength and more about creating a system where good choices become natural. A disciplined life doesn't depend on extraordinary effort; it grows out of ordinary actions repeated faithfully until they become part of who you are.

Think about it like water dripping on a stone. A single drop doesn't seem powerful. It looks insignificant, almost forgettable. But drop after drop, day after day, year after year, that steady rhythm carves valleys into solid rock. Discipline works the same way. It is not one grand gesture that changes a life but the quiet repetition of small steps that eventually reshape character. What feels invisible today becomes undeniable tomorrow.

That's why discipline cannot be reduced to occasional actions. It isn't about what a child does once in a while; it is about who they are becoming. A disciplined SPOILED Kid doesn't just say, "I saved money this week." They begin to believe, "I am a saver." They don't just say, "I finished my chores." They embrace, "I am responsible." They don't just say, "I studied." They own, "I am a learner." The shift from action to identity is where discipline moves from temporary effort to lasting transformation.

In our home, we constantly remind our daughters that every small act of discipline is a vote for the person they want to become. Each choice is like casting a ballot in the election of their identity. If they practice kindness, they are voting to become compassionate. If they complete their homework on time, they are voting to become consistent. If they show up to help with the food truck when it's hot and tiring, they are voting to become dependable. One vote by itself doesn't decide the outcome. But over time, the ballots add up. The majority wins. And little by little, their character takes shape.

Discipline is built one vote at a time. One choice at a time. One drop of water at a time. Over the days, the weeks, the years, those small actions carve out something stronger than stone: they carve out identity, confidence, and legacy. And this is the true genius of discipline—it doesn't just shape what children *do*; it shapes who they *are*.

The beauty of discipline is that it compounds. Just as a dollar placed in savings grows not only by what is added, but by the interest it earns over time, small acts of discipline build on themselves and multiply. The early steps may feel slow, almost invisible, but given time, they begin to produce results that are far greater than the effort that was put in. A disciplined life is never built in a day; it is built day by day. Just as money grows through compound interest, so do habits. A child who studies for fifteen minutes every night may not see the benefit in a week, but give it a year and they will be far ahead of where they started. A child who saves a small amount each week may not feel wealthy right away, but give it five years and they will have something significant.

When our daughters save money from the café, their jars may look unimpressive at first—a few bills and coins stacked together. But discipline teaches them that the first few dollars are the hardest, because the growth seems so small. Once a habit is established, however, the growth accelerates. A saver doesn't just fill a jar; they learn to think like an investor. They begin to ask not only, *How much do I have?* but *How can I make it grow?* That simple act of disciplined saving creates a ripple effect that reshapes how they view money for the rest of their lives.

The same compounding effect is true in leadership. A child who practices discipline by taking responsibility at home—leading a sibling in chores, staying calm in conflict, or finishing a task without

DISCIPLINE

reminders—is casting votes for their identity as a leader. At first, it's small: leading at home or among friends. But over time, those small acts grow into the capacity to lead teams, organizations, and even communities. Leadership is rarely built in sudden leaps; it grows by compounding moments of discipline when no one is watching.

Learning, too, follows this pattern. Fifteen minutes of reading each night may not look impressive on day one. But stack those minutes over weeks and months, and suddenly a child has read dozens of books. The same principle applies to practicing a sport, learning an instrument, or mastering a new language. Discipline is what transforms scattered effort into stacked progress, turning knowledge into mastery.

And the compounding nature of discipline does not stop with individuals—it extends to families and legacies. Every disciplined choice a child makes adds strength not only to their own character but to the family name. When a child learns to save, the family becomes wealthier. When a child learns to lead, the family becomes stronger. When a child learns to serve with kindness and responsibility, the family becomes more influential. Over time, these choices build into a legacy of stability, resilience, and blessing that future generations can inherit.

This is why discipline cannot be underestimated. It is not glamorous. It is not dramatic. But it is unstoppable. Like interest that grows quietly in an account or water that carves valleys into stone, discipline compounds until the results are undeniable. One disciplined choice today may feel small, but multiplied over years, it becomes the foundation of wealth, wisdom, and generational legacy.

Discipline 7.4:

Shaping the Environmental

Discipline is not just about what's inside a child; it's also about what surrounds them. Environments shape choices. The soil matters as much as the seed. Even the most disciplined intentions can wither in the wrong conditions, while the right environment can make good choices feel almost effortless.

Think of it this way: if you plant a seed in dry, rocky ground, it may sprout, but it will struggle. Plant that same seed in rich soil, with access to sunlight and water, and it thrives with less strain. Children are no different. A child whose money jar is visible on the dresser, where they can see it grow day by day, is more likely to save than one who has to dig it out from the back of a drawer. A child with books sitting on their nightstand, covers facing outward, is more likely to read than one who has to rummage through a closet to find them. The environment does not replace discipline, but it amplifies it.

We saw this clearly when we wanted to encourage healthier eating habits in our family. We realized it wasn't enough to lecture our daughters about nutrition or tell them what not to eat. So we changed the environment. We stocked the kitchen with fruits, nuts, and smoothies. We put apples in a bowl right on the counter, within easy reach. We filled the fridge with colorful vegetables, prepped and ready to eat. And we limited the junk food in the house. Suddenly, discipline wasn't about resisting temptation; it was about leaning into what was available. The environment did the teaching for us.

The same principle applied when we wanted to encourage saving. We gave each daughter her own clear jar for money, placed in her room where it could be seen every day. At first, it was just a few coins rattling at the bottom. But soon, as they added more from chores or small sales at the café, they could see their progress stacking up. The jars became visual encouragement, a silent coach reminding them of their goal. It was no longer about abstract lessons on delayed gratification; the environment itself made saving natural.

Even schoolwork was easier when we adjusted the environment. For homework, we created a quiet corner with good lighting, a desk, and supplies within reach. No clutter, no distractions. The space became an invitation to focus. Compare that to trying to complete assignments in front of the TV or while sprawled on the couch. One environment made discipline feel forced, the other made it flow.

This is why environments matter so deeply: they whisper louder than words. They send subtle but powerful messages about what is possible, what is expected, and what is normal. When a guitar is placed on a stand in the living room, a child is more likely to pick it up than if it's hidden in its case in the attic. When a basketball is left by the door, it invites a quick game outside. When journals and pens are left on the table, they spark reflection. Each of these choices is a way of curating an environment where discipline grows like a plant in good soil.

But environments can work against us, too. A pantry stocked with soda and chips makes unhealthy choices automatic. A bedroom cluttered with screens makes sleep a battle. A life with no structure creates chaos that discipline alone can't fix. That's why parents play such a critical role in shaping spaces that serve as scaffolding for their children's discipline.

Our goal as parents is not to control our children but to design environments that support their growth. We can't walk every step for them, but we can build paths that make those steps easier to take. Just like gardeners prepare the soil, pull weeds, and water faithfully so plants can thrive, we prepare the spaces, rhythms, and systems so our children can develop the habits that will shape their character.

Because in the end, discipline is never just about willpower. It is about placement, positioning, and preparation. Put the seed in the right soil, and discipline won't just survive—it will flourish.

Discipline 7.5:

The Seeds of Discipline

Discipline may not feel glamorous at the moment. It's not always exciting to say no to instant rewards, admit mistakes, or keep grinding when nobody is watching. But discipline is like planting a seed in the soil—the work often begins in hidden places. You press the seed down into the dark earth, water it, and then you wait. Days pass, sometimes weeks, with no visible change. It looks as though nothing is happening. But beneath the surface, something powerful is taking place. Roots are stretching, anchoring the seed, preparing it to rise. Then, at last, stems break through the soil, and what was once invisible becomes undeniable.

This is exactly how discipline works in the life of a child. The daily practices, the consistent habits, the quiet choices to say "yes" to responsibility and "no" to temptation—none of it looks impressive at first. In fact, most of it is invisible. A child making their bed, turning in homework, or biting their tongue instead of lashing out doesn't look like transformation. But given time, patience, and intentional care, those actions grow into something much greater than the moment. Discipline, like a seed, produces freedom, fruit, and legacy.

Every disciplined life begins with small seeds. Seeds are simple, often overlooked, but packed with potential. In our family, the seeds of discipline look like: making the bed each morning, doing chores without complaint, finishing homework before play, setting aside money instead of spending it all, showing respect even when emotions run high. At first glance, these look like ordinary actions, but in truth they are seeds of greatness. We tell our daughters often: *"Don't despise the small things. Every oak tree begins as a seed."*

The early years of discipline are all about planting consistently. It's not the size of the seed that matters—it's the habit of planting. A seed left in a packet will never grow. A seed planted once in dry soil will wither. But a seed planted faithfully, watered daily, and guarded carefully will always bear fruit in time. And here's where we as parents must be honest: sometimes, we don't plant consistently. Sometimes we scatter seeds and then forget to water them.

We have had to admit this in our own home. At times, we "spoiled" our kids not in the empowering SPOILED way we describe in this book but in the unhealthy sense of overindulgence. We let things slide that should have been addressed. We allowed excuses when we should have insisted on accountability. We gave in to comfort when we should have modeled consistency. And because of that, our children reflected back to us what we had sown. When we were inconsistent, they were inconsistent. When we failed to follow through, so did they. When we complained, grumbled, or looked defeated under pressure, our children caught those habits too. Seeds don't only grow when planted on purpose—they also grow when planted by accident.

That realization has been humbling. It reminded us that discipline is not only something we teach; it is something we must embody. Children do not simply listen to what we say; they study how we live. If we lose patience quickly, so will they. If we give up easily, so will they. If we lack follow-through, they will mirror it. But when we remain steadfast in the face of challenges, when we model consistency even in the small things, when we choose positivity and perseverance instead of defeat—our children learn discipline not as a lecture but as a way of life.

Parents, we must remain committed to the process, even when progress feels slow. We must plant seeds of discipline in our homes every single day, trusting that in due season, they will grow. It is not perfection that raises disciplined children, but persistence. Without a consistent representation of discipline in us, our children will not learn this vital skill. But when they see us living it, even in struggle, they will inherit a legacy of roots and fruit that will sustain them long after we are gone.

We can remember one Saturday morning when

our family was working the Black Leaf Vegan food truck. It was hot, very very hot, the line was long, and things weren't running smoothly. The generator had cut out again, orders were piling up, and it was extremely frustrating. The words, we thought under our breath, "Oh my God, this is too much today." We didn't think much of it in the moment, but later, we overheard one of my daughters sighing while taking orders. She muttered almost the exact same words that she heard from her parents: "This is too much today, I can't do this."

It stopped us cold. She wasn't just imitating our words—she was imitating our spirit. Our frustration had planted a seed, and she was already watering it.

That moment humbled us, because it reminded us that discipline isn't just what we demand of our children—it's what we demonstrate. When we allowed ourselves to complain, she learned that giving in to discouragement was acceptable. But when we took a deep breath, reset our attitude, and reminded the team, "We've got this, one order at a time," she mirrored that too. She straightened up, smiled at the next customer, and got back to work with new energy.

Children catch what we plant. Seeds of complaint grow into weeds of discouragement. Seeds of persistence grow into trees of resilience. And just as quickly as my daughter picked up my frustration, she picked up my renewed discipline.

That day taught me again that our children are the soil where our habits fall—good or bad. What we plant in them, they will grow.

Discipline 7.6:

The Growth of the Seed

One of the most important truths about discipline is that growth almost always happens underground before it is visible above. Roots stretch deep before branches ever reach wide. The unseen work is the most essential work, because without strong roots, any tree will topple at the first storm.

That's why we cannot rush discipline. We may not see the results immediately, and that can be frustrating. A child may resist routines, fight responsibilities, or seem careless about money, time, or effort. On the surface it looks like nothing is taking hold. But beneath the soil of daily practice, roots are forming. Every time they come back to the habit—even reluctantly—the roots go deeper. Every time they choose responsibility over excuses, even in small ways, the roots push further into the ground.

This is where parents must trust the process. Just as farmers do not dig up seeds every week to see if they are growing, we cannot expect instant fruit from every lesson. Our job is to keep planting, keep watering, and keep protecting the soil. The roots will come.

We often think of our first rental property. When we won it at the tax sale, it was not a shining piece of real estate—it was a broken-down house that demanded vision, patience, and sacrifice. The results weren't instant. We spent months fixing it up, managing costs, and working weekends when it would have been easier to relax. Our daughters didn't always understand why we chose to work instead of "having fun." They saw the surface—the sweat, the sacrifice, the setbacks. What they couldn't see at first were the roots: passive income, ownership, and a legacy that would keep giving long after the paint dried and the tools were put away.

The same principle applies to them. When they save money instead of spending it, when they show up to do a chore without complaining, when they push through homework before play, it may not feel like much. But those choices are roots. Roots that will sustain them when life gets hard, roots that will stabilize them when storms come, roots that will allow them to grow tall and bear fruit in their season.

Roots are patient. Roots are persistent. Roots are invisible—until one day, they aren't. The tree that was once fragile becomes unshakable, and the child who once resisted discipline becomes the adult who thrives because of it.

Discipline 7.7:

The Root System of Discipline

Every strong tree depends on its root system. Roots are unseen, but they anchor the tree, nourish it, and prepare it to endure storms and seasons. Without roots, the tallest trunk falls. With roots, even the smallest sapling can grow into a mighty oak. In the same way, a disciplined life grows out of invisible foundations. What we see on the surface—confidence, success, leadership, wealth—is only possible because of the roots underneath.

Here are four roots every SPOILED child must cultivate:
1. Financial Roots (Saving and Stewardship)

The first root of discipline is learning how to manage resources. Before a child can one day invest in businesses, buy homes, or build wealth, they must first practice the simple discipline of saving. A visible jar of coins, a small savings account, or even setting aside part of an allowance—these are roots pushing into the soil. It may not look impressive today, but underground it is building habits of stewardship that will carry them for a lifetime. We think of the nights we emptied tips from the café into jars for the girls. At first, they wanted to spend it right away, but we reminded them: "Every dollar saved is a root planted." Over time, those roots became thicker, deeper, and stronger—leading to opportunities for travel, learning, and eventually investments of their own.

2. Leadership Roots (Responsibility and Service)

    Leadership does not appear overnight. It grows underground through small acts of responsibility. When a child learns to keep their word, help a sibling, or finish what they start, those actions become roots that one day grow into leadership.

    We remember watching one of our daughters guide her younger sister through homework. She didn't know it, but she was strengthening leadership roots. She was learning patience, communication, and accountability. Years later, those roots will grow into the ability to lead teams, inspire communities, and stand tall when others look for guidance.

3. Learning Roots (Habits of Growth)

    Knowledge itself is fruit, but the roots are in the habits of learning. A child who reads fifteen minutes a night, practices multiplication tables consistently, or writes daily in a journal is not just collecting facts. They are building roots of curiosity and perseverance.

When we travel, we require our daughters to keep journals, even when they would rather just explore. Sometimes they resist, but we remind them that journaling is a root—it keeps them grounded in reflection, memory, and growth. Those habits form roots that will sustain their academic and personal lives far beyond childhood.

4. Character Roots (Integrity and Resilience)

Perhaps the deepest roots are the ones tied to character. Money, success, and recognition will all come and go, but integrity and resilience keep a person standing when everything else shakes. These roots are formed when children tell the truth even when it costs them, when they try again after failure, when they show respect even when upset.

We think of moments when our daughters faced disappointment—losing a game, missing out on a reward, or not getting what they wanted right away. Each time we encouraged them to try again, to speak kindly, to hold themselves with dignity, roots were stretching underground. One day, those roots will hold them steady in far greater storms.

The world often celebrates the fruit—the visible success. We applaud the child who wins the award, the student who earns the scholarship, the entrepreneur who makes the money. But fruit cannot grow without roots. The deeper the roots, the sweeter and stronger the fruit.

And here's the truth: roots don't just sustain one tree. They expand underground, connecting and strengthening entire groves. In the same way, when a child grows roots of discipline in finance, leadership, learning, and character, they don't just bless themselves—they strengthen their family, their community, and their future generations.

Discipline is root work. It is patient, hidden, and often uncelebrated. But it is also the quiet genius that makes greatness possible.

Discipline 7.8:

The Fruit of Discipline

Fruit is the visible evidence of discipline. It's the tangible reward after the long wait, the proof that sacrifice wasn't wasted. Fruit is the "A" on the test after weeks of studying when others quit early. It's the money saved that turns into a plane ticket, unlocking the chance to see the world. It's the stronger body built one workout at a time, even on days when the couch felt more inviting. It's the restored relationship that came because someone held their tongue and chose patience instead of anger.

For our family, fruit has taken on many forms. It has looked like the joy of unlocking the doors to our café for the very first time, knowing it was the result of countless disciplined days in a food truck, through sweat, setbacks, and perseverance. It has looked like watching our daughters walk confidently on foreign soil, speaking Spanish words that once tripped their tongues, proof that daily study and practice produced fluency. It has looked like the quiet but powerful moment when one of them admitted a mistake without being pressed, embodying the fruit of honesty, patience, and integrity.

Fruit is sweet. But it is also revealing. The harvest shows exactly what kind of seed was planted, what kind of soil was tended, and what kind of roots were nurtured. If weeds were allowed to grow, the fruit will show it. If care and consistency were given, the fruit will show that too. Fruit is the evidence of what has been happening underground all along.

And here is the miracle of discipline: fruit does not exist only for the tree that produces it. Fruit always carries more potential. It not only nourishes the one who eats it, it carries within it the seeds for future harvests. A disciplined child doesn't just grow one strong tree; they have the power to create an orchard.

When one of our daughters learns to save money, she gains financial freedom—but that's not the end. She becomes a seed planter. She can teach her sisters, influence her friends, and one day guide her own children. The fruit of her discipline contains seeds that will multiply far beyond her.

Think of how trees reproduce. An apple tree doesn't stop with a single apple. Over its lifetime it produces thousands, and within each apple are more seeds capable of producing more trees. Discipline works the same way. A habit practiced in one life rarely stays there. It spreads, multiplies, and becomes part of the fabric of families, communities, and cultures.

This is how legacy is built. A disciplined parent models persistence, and a child picks it up. That child teaches it to their children, and suddenly you have generations rooted in resilience. A family learns to manage money wisely, and within a few decades that discipline has transformed into homes owned, businesses established, and opportunities created for countless others. The fruit of discipline doesn't just satisfy for a season; it sustains for a lifetime and multiplies into eternity.

That is why we must never despise the small beginnings, the unseen roots, or the slow growth. In time, the harvest will come. And when it does, it will be more than sweet fruit for ourselves—it will be seeds for the world, gifts to plant in the lives of others, multiplying into orchards that will bless generations yet to be born.

Discipline 7.9:

Discipline as Legacy

The long game of discipline is freedom. It is freedom from the trap of impulsive living, freedom from wasted potential, and freedom from being controlled by distractions. It is freedom to focus, freedom to finish, and freedom to flourish. A disciplined child grows into an adult who is equipped not only to manage their own life but to multiply their impact in the lives of others. Their steady habits magnify creativity, their patience deepens leadership, and their focus strengthens entrepreneurship. Discipline is not chains. It is wings. It is not the loss of freedom but the very path that makes freedom possible.

Think of a seed. At first glance, it appears small, insignificant, even buried. But being buried is not the same as being restricted—it is being positioned. In time, that seed grows roots, pushes upward, becomes a tree, and eventually bears fruit. And within every piece of fruit are seeds that can produce more trees. That is the miracle of discipline: the choice to study today, to save today, to endure today may look small, but it multiplies into something that stretches far beyond the present moment.

DISCIPLINE

This is how disciplined children become disciplined adults. This is how a disciplined family becomes a disciplined community. And this is how one family's orchard of discipline can, over time, expand into a forest of legacy that cannot be uprooted. Discipline doesn't just sustain a single generation—it creates a culture. It builds habits into the DNA of a family line.

In this way, discipline is more than personal success—it is legacy. It ensures that what is built does not collapse when tested, that what is earned is not squandered when temptations rise, and that what is planted produces fruit for generations. A disciplined SPOILED Kid is not just a child who works hard today; they are a leader who will carry stability, wisdom, and resilience into every space they touch tomorrow.

We imagine our family a hundred years from now. Perhaps it is our great-grandchildren walking into homes they own, running businesses that were once only ideas scribbled on napkins, tending to our 300 acre farm, expanding our family compound, or traveling the world with ease because the seeds of saving, hard work, and perseverance were planted long before them. They may never know all the sweat, the choices, the sacrifices that built the soil they now stand on— but they will eat the fruit. They will rest in the s hade of trees planted by parents, grandparents, and great-grandparents who chose discipline. That is a legacy!

And so, though discipline is often quiet and

unseen, it is the genius behind greatness. It is the steady rhythm beneath every achievement, the invisible scaffolding that holds up every dream. To raise a disciplined child is to raise not only a successful individual but a multiplier of success, a builder of legacies, and a gift to the world.

The ultimate vision is not just raising a single disciplined child, but cultivating a forest. Imagine walking through an orchard your family planted—trees stretching high, roots deep, branches heavy with fruit, shade offering rest to anyone who passes by, and seeds dropping to the ground to begin the cycle again. That is the vision of discipline in the SPOILED framework: abundance, sustainability, and blessing that reaches far beyond ourselves.

We are not raising kids only for the present moment. We are raising generations. Every disciplined choice today—to study instead of scroll, to save instead of spend, to serve instead of complain, to build instead of quit—is a seed for the future. Just as a forest provides stability for the land, the disciplined lives of our children will provide stability for our family name, our community, and beyond. The forest of legacy begins with a single seed, planted faithfully today.

When you raise a disciplined SPOILED Kid, you are raising someone who has the structure to carry vision, the strength to handle adversity, and the wisdom to build wealth that lasts. They will not be tossed around by every trend or temptation. They will walk with confidence, grounded in the quiet power of consistency.

And in the end, that's the gift discipline gives: not just success for today, but stability for tomorrow. Not just survival, but legacy.

Conclusion:

Living the SPOILED Legacy

The SPOILED Kid mindset isn't only about managing money—it's about cultivating a lifestyle where every action, resource, and decision aligns with a greater vision of abundance. This framework is not a checklist to complete, but a way of being that touches every area of life. For example, when deciding to purchase a property, a SPOILED Kid will save funds strategically (Savers), build a business or skill set to fuel the investment (Producers), aim to own the asset fully (Owners), research the market extensively to ensure wise stewardship (Investors), and step confidently into leadership when making decisions (Leaders). They see obstacles not as deterrents but as opportunities to innovate (Entrepreneurs), and they remain consistent and resilient in carrying out their plans (Disciplined).

Each letter of SPOILED reinforces the others, creating a cycle of growth that is not only sustainable but generational. Saving fuels ownership. Producing leads to investing. Leadership calls for discipline. Entrepreneurship demands resilience. These principles do not stand alone; they weave together into a life marked by abundance, vision, and purpose.

This mindset produces more than financial wealth. It fosters self-reliance, resilience, character, and a deep understanding of what true wealth really means. True wealth is not only measured in dollars but in freedom, in relationships, in opportunities created, and in the impact left behind. A SPOILED child learns early that every investment—whether of time, energy, money, or love—is a seed planted toward a future harvest. By encouraging children and young people to adopt this mindset, we are giving them tools not just for financial success but for a life that is rich, grounded, and fulfilling, one where every decision aligns with their broader vision of legacy.

Our family's journey of living the SPOILED lifestyle has not been easy. It has required sacrifice, patience, and hard lessons learned along the way. But it has been worth every struggle. Watching our children overcome challenges brings us immeasurable delight. Seeing them navigate new experiences, or take calculated risks without fear, reminds us that the seeds we planted are growing. Having a front row seat to the movie of their lives—watching the script being written by them instead of simply reenacting the old scripts handed down from previous generations—often has us on the edge of our seats. And yet, even in moments of suspense, we are confident that the ending and every sequel after will be fantastic, because their story is being written with discipline, vision, and courage.

The legacy of the SPOILED framework is not confined to one family or one generation. It is a gift designed to multiply. A child raised with these principles will pass them on to their children. A disciplined saver will raise producers. An owner will inspire investors. A leader will empower entrepreneurs. A disciplined child will raise a disciplined community. And in time, what began as one seed, planted in one family, will grow into an orchard of abundance, stability, and freedom that blesses generations yet unborn.

This is the long game of the SPOILED lifestyle. It is not about raising children who are simply prepared for the present moment but about raising legacy makers. When children embrace this mindset, they not only secure their own futures, they build foundations for others. They will become leaders who stand tall when others bow, investors who multiply resources when others consume, and visionaries who build roads where others see barriers.

And so, as we close this book, we leave you with this truth: the SPOILED framework is not a theory—it is a way of life. It is a call to action for families, parents, mentors, and communities to plant seeds of abundance, cultivate habits of growth, and reap harvests of generational wealth and wisdom. To raise a SPOILED Kid is to raise a child who is free, a child who is focused, a child who is prepared to leave the world better than they found it.

DISCIPLINE

The orchard is waiting. The soil is ready. The seeds are in your hands. Plant them faithfully. Water them consistently. Nurture them patiently. And if you are anything like us, you won't always get it right. But with determination, you will watch as your children, your family, and your community reap the fruit of a legacy that cannot be uprooted.

The SPOILED Edict

We believe every child carries seeds of greatness.

We believe discipline is not chains—it is wings.

We believe wealth is more than money—it is freedom, wisdom, and love.

We believe in raising children who do not wait for opportunity—they create it.

We believe that small habits become roots, roots become trees, and trees become orchards.

We believe in saving not just for ourselves, but for generations.

We believe in producing with excellence, owning with integrity, and investing with vision.

We believe in leading with courage, serving with humility, and persevering with resilience.

We believe that every challenge is a classroom, every failure is a seed, and every success is fruit to be shared.

DISCIPLINE

We believe the SPOILED lifestyle is not indulgence—
it is intentional legacy.

And so we raise our children with this truth:

They are Savers.
They are Producers.
They are Owners.
They are Investors.
They are Leaders.
They are Entrepreneurs.
They are Disciplined.

We are not just raising kids.

We are raising legacy makers.
We are raising freedom builders.
We are raising world changers.

This is the SPOILED way.
This is our gift to the world.

Derrick & Taria Slack

Derrick & Taria Slack are visionary entrepreneurs, educators, and authors dedicated to transforming families, communities, and future generations through the power of mindset, ownership, and intentional living. They have traveled to nearly 50 countries worldwide sharing their groundbreaking framework they created that equips families with practical tools and timeless principles to build legacy, foster leadership, and cultivate abundance.

The Slacks are also the co-founders and owners of Black Leaf Vegan, an award-winning plant-based café and food trucks in Indianapolis known for its mission to heal and empower communities through food, culture, and education. What began as a bold venture during the pandemic has blossomed into a thriving culinary and cultural hub, inspiring healthier lifestyles and collective well-being.

With decades of combined experience in education, leadership, and entrepreneurship, the Slacks bring a deeply personal and purpose-driven approach to everything they do. Their work—writing books, international speaking engagements, designing youth and wellness programs, leading workshops and building businesses—reflects a shared commitment to legacy-building, family empowerment, and creating opportunities that outlast a single lifetime. Derrick and Taria are on a mission to help families everywhere live intentionally, build wealth purposefully, and thrive generationally.

DISCIPLINE

www.ingramcontent.com/pod-product-compliance
Lightning Source LLC
Chambersburg PA
CBHW071855290426
44110CB00013B/1156